REPTILES

D0905280

For: Austin Michael
Berthiaume

ALLIGATOR
SNAPPING TURTLE

STARRED
TORTOISE

CORN SNAKE

CHAMELEON

A FIREFLY POCKET GUIDE

REPTILES

Written by
MARK LAMBERT

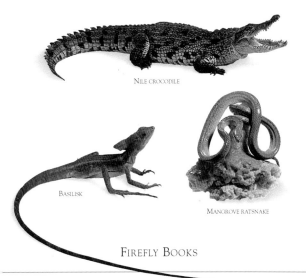

NILE CROCODILE

BASILISK

MANGROVE RATSNAKE

FIREFLY BOOKS

A DORLING KINDERSLEY BOOK

Project editors	Leo Vita-Finzi
	John Mapps
Art editor	Mark Regardsoe
Design assistant	Tanya Tween
Senior editor	Alastair Dougall
Senior art editors	Carole Oliver
	Sarah Crouch
Picture research	Neil Aldridge
Production	Kate Oliver

First published in Canada in 1997
by Firefly Books Ltd.
3860 Victoria Park Avenue
Willowdale, Ontario M2H 3K1

Canadian Cataloguing in Publication Data

Lambert, Mark, 1946-
Reptiles
(Firefly pocket guides)
Includes index.
ISBN 1-55209-173-2
1. Reptiles   I. Title   II. Series

QL644.L35 1997   597.9   C97-930916-6

Color reproduction by Colourscan, Singapore
Printed and bound in Italy by L.E.G.O.

CONTENTS

HOW TO USE THIS BOOK

These pages show you how to use *Pockets: Reptiles*.
The book is divided into six sections. The main
sections consist of information about four reptile
groups. There is an introductory section at the front
of the book and a reference section at the back, as
well as a glossary and comprehensive index.

ALL ABOUT REPTILES
The reptiles in this book
are presented in four
sections: chelonians,
crocodiles and alligators,
lizards, and snakes.
Within each section
you will find detailed
information on the most
important species.

Corner coding

Heading

Introduction

Label

CROCODILES AND ALLIGATORS

ALLIGATORS AND CAIMANS

ALLIGATORS AND CAIMANS have shorter snouts than
crocodiles, and they live solely in freshwater. There
are two species of alligator, the American alligator
and the rare Chinese
alligator. The various species
of caiman are all found in
Americas, ranging from
Mexico to South America
and the Caribbean.

SLOW DOWN, LIVE LONGER
Alligators are more sluggish than
crocodiles. This may be why they
live longer – there are records of
alligators living for up to 50 years.
Widespread hunting, however,
severely threatens the animal's
survival in the wild.

SKULL
An alligator's skull is
shorter and broader than a
crocodile's. The toothsome
jaws can carry young with
surprising delicacy.

HUNTED DOWN
American
alligators can grow to
20 ft (6 m) in length, but because
of hunting it is rare nowadays to find
individuals longer than 10 ft (3 m).

HEADING
The heading
describes the overall
subject of the page.
This page is about
alligators and
caimans. Sometimes
the same subject will
continue over
several pages.

CORNER CODING
The corners of the
main section pages are
colour coded to
remind you which
section you are in.

- [ ] CHELONIANS
- [ ] CROCODILES AND
  ALLIGATORS
- [ ] LIZARDS
- [ ] SNAKES

INTRODUCTION
The introduction provides
an overview of the
subject. After reading this,
you should have a clear
idea of what the pages
are about.

CAPTIONS AND
ANNOTATIONS
Each illustration has a
caption. Annotations, in
italics, point out features
of an illustration, and
usually have leader lines.

RUNNING HEADS

These remind you which section you are in. The top of the left-hand page gives the section name. The top of the right-hand page gives the subject.

LABELS

For extra clarity, some pictures have labels. These may give extra information about the picture, or identify a picture if this is not obvious from the text.

FEATURE BOXES

These boxes provide additional information, such as how a snake hatches or how a constrictor eats its prey.

Running head

Annotation

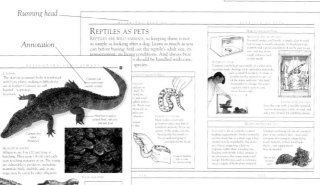

REFERENCE SECTION

The reference section pages are yellow and appear at the back of the book. On these you will find useful facts and figures, including reptile records and names and addresses of zoos.

FACT BOXES

Many pages have fact boxes. These provide at-a-glance information about the subject, such as the names of the only two poisonous lizards.

INDEX

The index lists every subject and type of reptile covered in the book, including the scientific names of the reptiles mentioned. Look up the index when you want to find information on a particular topic.

INTRODUCTION TO REPTILES

WHAT IS A REPTILE?

PAINTING OF MEDUSA

MEDUSA
Throughout history, reptiles have been feared. Medusa, a monster from Greek mythology, had snakes for hair.

LIKE FISH, amphibians, birds, and mammals, reptiles are vertebrates (have backbones). But what makes them different from fish and amphibians is that they are basically land animals – they do not have to live in or keep returning to water. And unlike birds and mammals, they are cold-blooded. That is, their bodies remain at the same temperature as their surroundings.

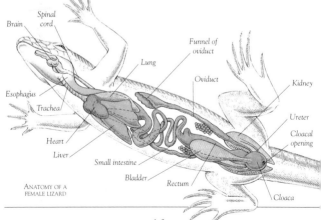

Brain

Spinal cord

Funnel of oviduct

Lung

Oviduct

Kidney

Esophagus

Trachea

Ureter

Cloacal opening

Heart

Liver

Small intestine

Bladder

Rectum

Cloaca

ANATOMY OF A FEMALE LIZARD

SEEN FROM
THE OUTSIDE
Lizards are typical
reptiles. The crested
water dragon, shown
below, is found in Asia.
It has scaly skin that is
waterproof – thus retaining
moisture inside the reptile's body.

Long tail for balance

Eye

GLASSY STARE
Snakes and some
lizards do not have
movable eyelids. Instead
the eye is covered with a
transparent membrane, called the
spectacle, that protects the eye
from damage.

Long toes for support

Scaly skin

CRESTED WATER DRAGON

EGG LAYERS
Some reptiles
produce active
young, but most
species lay eggs.
Here a young rat-
snake is hatching.

RATSNAKE

INSIDE A REPTILE
A reptile has a small
brain and a heart with three
chambers (a human heart has
four). The cloaca, a chamber at
the rear of the gut, is used by
the bladder when excreting and
by the reproductive system
during sexual reproduction.

AN EXTRA EYELID

Crocodiles have
three eyelids.
There are two
above and below
the eye. An extra
see-through lid
covers the eye
from the inner
corner to protect
the surface of the
eye under water.

REPTILE GROUPS

REPTILES FIRST APPEARED about 340 million years ago, during the Carboniferous period (see diagram). Their ancestors were amphibians, but the first reptiles could breed without having to return to water. Today, four main groups remain: turtles and tortoises (chelonians), snakes and lizards, crocodilians, and the tuatara.

GIANT SEA SNAKE

PALAEOPHIS
Snakes first appeared in the late Jurassic. Palaeophis was an ancient sea snake.

MODERN PYTHON
These vertebrae are from a python that is four times smaller than Palaeophis.

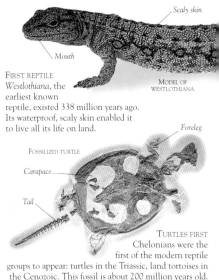

Scaly skin

Mouth

FIRST REPTILE
Westlothiana, the earliest known reptile, existed 338 million years ago. Its waterproof, scaly skin enabled it to live all its life on land.

MODEL OF
WESTLOTHIANA

Foreleg

FOSSILIZED TURTLE

Carapace

Tail

TURTLES FIRST
Chelonians were the first of the modern reptile groups to appear: turtles in the Triassic, land tortoises in the Cenozoic. This fossil is about 200 million years old.

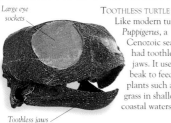

Large eye sockets

TOOTHLESS TURTLE
Like modern turtles, *Puppigerus*, a Cenozoic sea turtle, had toothless jaws. It used its beak to feed on plants such as sea-grass in shallow coastal waters.

Toothless jaws

REPTILE GROUP FACTS
• Rhynchocephalians were common in the Triassic. Today, the only one left is the tuatara.
• Mammal-like reptiles appeared in the Permian. During the Triassic they gave rise to the first mammals.

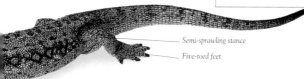

Semi-sprawling stance

Five-toed feet

REPTILE EVOLUTION
This diagram shows the evolution of reptiles. The column on the left shows when they existed and how many millions of years ago that was.

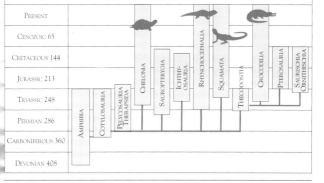

	AMPHIBIA	COTYLOSAURIA	PELYCOSAURIA THERAPSIDA	CHELONIA	SAUROPTERYGIA	ICHTHYOSAURIA	RHYNCHOCEPHALIA	SQUAMATA	THECODONTIA	CROCODILIA	PTEROSAURIA	SAURISCHIA ORNITHISCHIA
PRESENT												
CENOZOIC 65												
CRETACEOUS 144												
JURASSIC 213												
TRIASSIC 248												
PERMIAN 286												
CARBONIFEROUS 360												
DEVONIAN 408												

PREHISTORIC REPTILES

THE FIRST REPTILES encountered
no competition for the wide
range of land habitats
available. Over millions
of years they adapted
to every possible type
of lifestyle and diet.
Some of them even
learned to fly. Others
returned to living in
the sea.

*The "sail"
was probably
used to help
control body
temperature*

DIMETRODON

SAIL BACK
Dimetrodon was a
mammal-like reptile of the
Permian period. Its relatives
were the ancestors of
modern mammals.

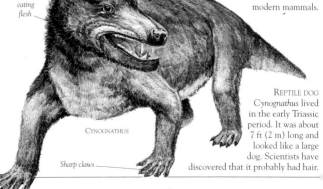

*Fangs and
sharp cheek-
teeth for
eating
flesh*

CYNOGNATHUS

Sharp claws

REPTILE DOG
Cynognathus lived
in the early Triassic
period. It was about
7 ft (2 m) long and
looked like a large
dog. Scientists have
discovered that it probably had hair.

BACK TO THE SEA
In the Jurassic and Cretaceous periods, some reptiles returned to living in water, but this time they chose the sea; there were invertebrates and fish to eat. Plesiosaurs had long necks and their limbs had become paddles.

REPTILE DOLPHINS
Ichthyosaurs were the most fishlike of reptiles. They were the same size – and ate the same food – as modern dolphins. Like many of today's fish, they used their tail to propel themselves and steered with their fins.

PLESIOSAUR

Dolphinlike snout

Powerful tail for swimming

ICHTHYOSAUR

Paddles for steering and braking

GIANT SEA LIZARDS
Mosasaurs were huge, measuring about 49 ft (15 m) in length. They preyed on fish and ammonites (a type of shellfish), crushing the shells in their powerful jaws.

MOSASAUR

1 7

More prehistoric reptiles

During the Jurassic and Cretaceous periods, reptiles ruled the land. Among these reptiles were the dinosaurs ("terrible lizards"). Some dinosaurs were gentle herbivores; others were ferocious carnivores. At the same time, a number of reptiles adapted to life in the air, 100 million years before flying birds appeared.

RHAMPHORHYNCIDS
The first flying reptiles, or pterosaurs, appeared during the Triassic period. *Rhamphorhynchus* and its relatives were Jurassic pterosaurs. They had long tails, curved snouts, and jaws with teeth. *Rhamphorynchus* may have used its teeth for spearing fish.

Claws on wings

Vane on tail for steering

Hairy body

RHAMPHORHYNCHUS

Throat pouch – possibly for holding fish

GLIDERS ANCIENT AND MODERN
Pterosaurs probably could not fly like birds. Instead, they launched themselves from cliffs and glided through the air, using updrafts – just like modern hang-gliders. The largest pterosaurs, such as *Pteranodon*, had wingspans of 26 ft (8 m) or more.

Tail may have aided balance while eating

PTERANODON AND HANG-GLIDER

Strong neck to support the huge head

Skin stretched between elongated fingers and the body, forming wings

Tyrannosaurus moved around on its massive hind legs

TYRANNOSAURUS

LIZARD TYRANT
Standing taller than a giraffe and weighing about 98 tons (100 tonnes), *Tyrannosaurus* was a two-legged carnivore with teeth up to 7 in (18 cm) long.

Tough hide helped protect against predators

Bony club to deter predators

EUOPLOCEPHALUS

EUOPLOCEPHALUS
Ankylosaurs, such as *Euoplocephalus*, needed protection from their carnivorous relatives. The tanklike ankylosaurs developed an armoured covering of bony plates and knobs. Some of them had clublike tails.

GENTLE GIANTS
Brachiosaurus and its relatives were huge but only ate vegetation. Its long neck, balanced by a long tail, enabled it to reach into high branches inaccessible to other creatures.

Massive legs to support the body's great weight

BRACHIOSAURUS

PREHISTORIC FACTS

• *Brachiosaurus* would have eaten 882 lb (400 kg) of food a day.

• Large carnivorous dinosaurs may have been warm-blooded.

• The fastest dinosaurs could run at up to 50 mph (80 km/h).

SCALY SKIN

REPTILES TYPICALLY have skins covered in overlapping, horny scales. They act as a waterproof covering and help retain precious body moisture.

In some reptiles, the scales form an armored protection. As a reptile grows, its old skin becomes too small and starts to wear out. A new skin replaces it.

ARMORED ALLIGATOR
Like all crocodilians, this Chinese alligator is covered in large, tough, partly ossified (turned into bone) scales. As it grows, the scales flake off and are replaced by new ones.

SECTION THROUGH SKIN

Scales

Upper layer of skin (epidermis)

Lower layer of skin (dermis)

Scales form in the epidermis. They are made mostly of keratin – the same substance found in hair and nails.

Each time a new piece is added, the oldest one falls off the end

WARNING RATTLE
A rattlesnake's rattle is made up of hollow pieces of keratin formed at the end of the tail. A new segment is added when the snake sheds its skin.

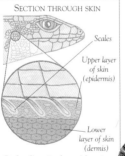

The rattle warns off attackers

Old skin
peeling off

SCALY SKIN FACTS
• A reptile grows throughout its life.
• The crests and spines sported by some lizards are formed from scales.
• Turtle shells are made of bony plates covered in horny material.

SHEDDING SNAKESKIN
A snake sheds its skin in one piece, beginning at the head. A new skin, complete with scales, has already formed underneath, and when the process is finished an entire transparent skin is left.

New skin

A SHED SNAKESKIN

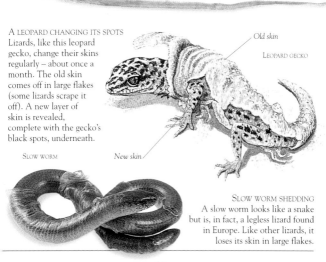

A LEOPARD CHANGING ITS SPOTS
Lizards, like this leopard gecko, change their skins regularly – about once a month. The old skin comes off in large flakes (some lizards scrape it off). A new layer of skin is revealed, complete with the gecko's black spots, underneath.

Old skin

LEOPARD GECKO

SLOW WORM

New skin

SLOW WORM SHEDDING
A slow worm looks like a snake but is, in fact, a legless lizard found in Europe. Like other lizards, it loses its skin in large flakes.

COLD-BLOODED CREATURES

REPTILES ARE DESCRIBED as cold-blooded. This does not mean that their blood is always cold. But, unlike birds and mammals, they do not make their own heat by using the chemical reactions in their bodies. Instead, a reptile relies on heat from the outside, and its body temperature goes up or down with the surrounding temperature.

CHILLING OUT
To cool, a reptile finds shade, or angles its body to expose the smallest possible area to the sun.

Reptiles warm up by basking in the sun

AGAMA LIZARD

COLD-BLOODED FACTS

• Scientists call "cold-blooded" animals poikilotherms or ectotherms.

• For digestion to take place, a high body temperature is needed. A snake that has just eaten may die if it is not warm enough.

WARMING UP
When a reptile starts to get too cold, it warms itself by basking in the sun, presenting as much of its body as possible to the sun's rays. By moving regularly between sun and shade, a reptile is able to maintain an almost constant body temperature.

REPTILE CIRCULATION

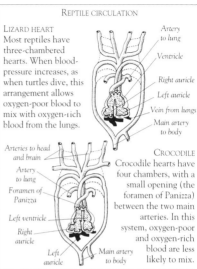

LIZARD HEART
Most reptiles have three-chambered hearts. When blood-pressure increases, as when turtles dive, this arrangement allows oxygen-poor blood to mix with oxygen-rich blood from the lungs.

Artery to lung

Ventricle

Right auricle

Left auricle

Vein from lungs

Main artery to body

CROCODILE
Crocodile hearts have four chambers, with a small opening (the foramen of Panizza) between the two main arteries. In this system, oxygen-poor and oxygen-rich blood are less likely to mix.

Arteries to head and brain

Artery to lung

Foramen of Panizza

Left ventricle

Right auricle

Left auricle

Main artery to body

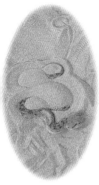

DIGGING IN
Shade is difficult to find in the desert. A sand viper solves this problem by wriggling its body down into the sand. If it did not do this it would literally fry in the heat.

Water evaporates from mouth

Like all reptiles, the crocodile cannot sweat to lose heat

OPEN-MOUTHED COOLING
One way of cooling is to let water evaporate from the body. A crocodile lies with its mouth open to let water evaporate from its mouth. American crocodiles lie in burrows when they get too hot. Other species cool down in water.

SENSES

MOST REPTILES have eyes
and ears. Snakes and
lizards also "taste"
their surroundings
using their tongues.
The tuatara, and
many lizards, also have a
light-sensitive organ on
their heads, which may be
important to temperature
regulation and to reproduction.

*Scaly skin contains
sensors that detect
touch, pain, heat,
and cold*

*Notched iris
with vertical slit*

*Heat-sensitive
pit*

SLIT EYES
A gecko is active mostly
at night and its eyes
are very sensitive. In
daylight, the iris of
each eye closes to a slit,
stopping too much light
from reaching the retina.
Notches in the iris allow
the animal to see.

HEAT SENSITIVE
A pit viper has a
heat-sensitive pit on
either side of its head.
Using these it can
follow the heat
trail of a warm-
blooded animal by
day or night. A pit
viper can detect
temperature changes of
0.002°C (0.002°F).

TEGU SENSES
A tegu lizard's well-developed eyes are designed for use in daylight and are protected by movable eyelids. Its eardrums are visible as small patches on the sides of its head behind the jaws. Its flicking, forked tongue is used, in conjunction with its Jacobson's organ, to "taste" the air.

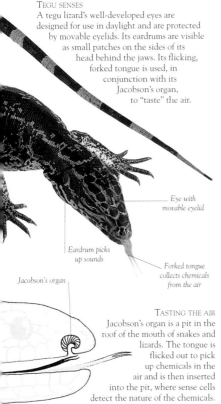

Eye with movable eyelid

Eardrum picks up sounds

Forked tongue collects chemicals from the air

Jacobson's organ

SWIVELING EYES
To see without being seen, a chameleon remains perfectly still, while swiveling its eyes to see in almost any direction. The eyes swivel independently of each other.

TASTING THE AIR
Jacobson's organ is a pit in the roof of the mouth of snakes and lizards. The tongue is flicked out to pick up chemicals in the air and is then inserted into the pit, where sense cells detect the nature of the chemicals.

SENSES FACTS

• A chameleon can use one eye to hunt and the other to watch out for predators.

• Most snakes "hear" by feeling vibrations through the ground; however, most lizards hear airborne sounds.

MOVEMENT

THE LEGS OF A typical reptile, such as a lizard, protrude sideways from its body. Heavier reptiles may require considerable physical effort to lift their bodies off the ground. Larger, land-based reptiles tend to move slowly, but smaller, lighter ones can be fast-moving and agile. Some reptiles, notably snakes, have dispensed with legs altogether.

GECKO

STICKY FEET
Geckos are small and light, and able to move rapidly. Pads on their feet have millions of tiny hooks that enable them to cling to smooth surfaces, even glass.

Fringelike scales on feet

SANDFISH

SWIMMING IN SAND
A sandfish (a type of skink) has fringelike scales on its feet to help it move on sand. It can also dive into the sand, wriggling like a snake.

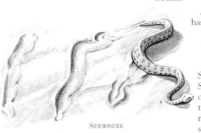

SIDEWINDER

SIDEWINDING
Some desert snakes move over the sand by looping their bodies sideways and moving in a series of sideways steps, known as sidewinding.

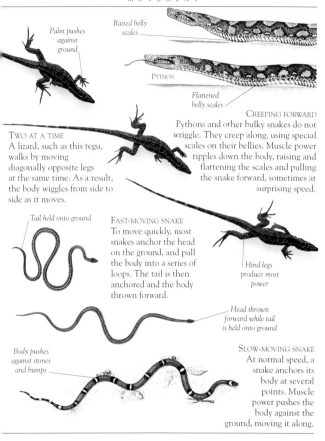

Palm pushes against ground

Raised belly scales

PYTHON

Flattened belly scales

CREEPING FORWARD
Pythons and other bulky snakes do not wriggle. They creep along, using special scales on their bellies. Muscle power ripples down the body, raising and flattening the scales and pulling the snake forward, sometimes at surprising speed.

TWO AT A TIME
A lizard, such as this tegu, walks by moving diagonally opposite legs at the same time. As a result, the body wiggles from side to side as it moves.

Tail held onto ground

FAST-MOVING SNAKE
To move quickly, most snakes anchor the head on the ground, and pull the body into a series of loops. The tail is then anchored and the body thrown forward.

Hind legs produce most power

Head thrown forward while tail is held onto ground

Body pushes against stones and bumps

SLOW-MOVING SNAKE
At normal speed, a snake anchors its body at several points. Muscle power pushes the body against the ground, moving it along.

Flying reptiles

Reptiles have never learned to fly like
bats or birds. The first "flying" reptiles, the
pterosaurs of the Triassic period, were gliding
animals rather
than fliers, and
the same is true of the
modern species that
have taken to the air.
Nevertheless, the ability to
glide can be very useful in
escaping quickly from predators
or simply moving swiftly from
one tree branch to the next in
the search for food.

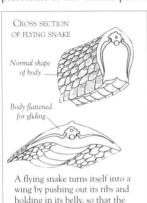

CROSS SECTION
OF FLYING SNAKE

*Normal shape
of body*

*Body flattened
for gliding*

A flying snake turns itself into a
wing by pushing out its ribs and
holding in its belly, so that the
body becomes flattened.

*Six or seven pairs of
ribs support skin flaps*

FLYING DRAGON
The "wings" of the flying dragon
of Southeast Asia are flaps of skin
supported by
elongated ribs.
They normally lie
folded against the
body, but can be
spread out wide
for gliding
flights.

*Limbs spread
out to help
steering*

Rough scales on the snake's belly help it climb trees

Flying snakes fly to escape predators, such as hawks

FLYING SNAKE
A flying snake uses its whole body as a "wing." It takes off from high in the treetops by uncoiling quickly and glides in a series of long curves. It steers by twisting its body from side to side. Flying snakes are found in Southeast Asia.

Webbed feet help in flying

GECKO AND FOOT
Flying geckos live in Asian rain forests. They glide by unfurling flaps of skin along the sides of the body, using the flattened tail to help steer. When at rest on tree bark, a flying gecko is very hard to see.

FLYING FACTS

• There are five species of Asian snake that are able to glide.

• There are unsubstantiated claims that large flying reptiles resembling pterosaurs still exist in the Jiundu swamp of Zambia.

COURTSHIP

LIKE ALL ANIMALS, reptiles need to attract members of the opposite sex in order to reproduce. They do this in various ways: by signals, colorful displays, or eye-catching ornaments, such as frills or crests.

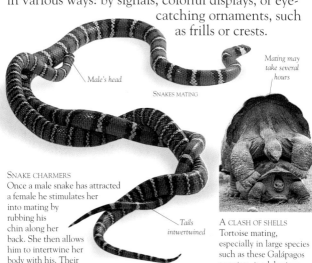

Male's head

SNAKES MATING

Mating may take several hours

SNAKE CHARMERS
Once a male snake has attracted a female he stimulates her into mating by rubbing his chin along her back. She then allows him to intertwine her body with his. Their cloacal openings meet, allowing sperm to pass from male to female.

Tails intwertwined

A CLASH OF SHELLS
Tortoise mating, especially in large species such as these Galápagos tortoises, is a laborious affair. The males roar during mating.

All anoles have very long tails

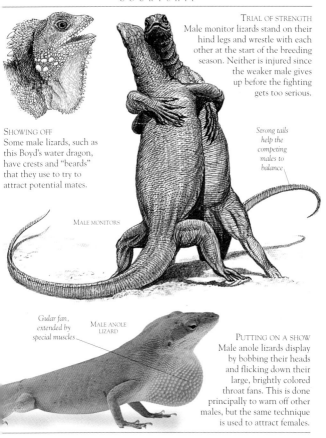

TRIAL OF STRENGTH
Male monitor lizards stand on their hind legs and wrestle with each other at the start of the breeding season. Neither is injured since the weaker male gives up before the fighting gets too serious.

Strong tails help the competing males to balance

SHOWING OFF
Some male lizards, such as this Boyd's water dragon, have crests and "beards" that they use to try to attract potential mates.

MALE MONITORS

Gular fan, extended by special muscles   MALE ANOLE LIZARD

PUTTING ON A SHOW
Male anole lizards display by bobbing their heads and flicking down their large, brightly colored throat fans. This is done principally to warn off other males, but the same technique is used to attract females.

NESTS AND EGGS

ANIMALS THAT TAKE CARE of their young usually have fewer offspring than those that leave their young to fend for themselves. Some reptiles, such as the marine turtles, lay thousands of eggs, but because they abandon them, only a few hatchlings reach maturity. A crocodile, on the other hand, guards not only her eggs but also her young for some time after they hatch. So a higher percentage of eggs and young survive.

ALLIGATOR NEST

ROTTEN NEST
A female American alligator builds a mound of mud and decaying vegetation, in which she lays 15 to 80 eggs. The heat produced by the rotting material incubates the eggs for two to three months.

The mother uncovers the eggs when they hatch

ON GUARD
The estuarine, or saltwater, crocodile of Southeast Asia and northern Australia builds a mound of leaves for her eggs. She builds her nest near water and shade so she can keep cool as she guards her offspring against predators, including lizards, herons, mongooses, turtles, and other crocodiles.

The female covers the nest with her body

SAFE IN MOTHER'S MOUTH
After baby Nile
crocodiles have
hatched, their mother
gathers as many as she
can in her mouth and
carries them to the
safety of a pool,
making several trips
to complete the task.
She remains to
defend her offspring.

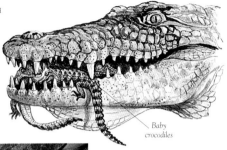

Baby crocodiles

GREEN TURTLE LAYING EGGS

NO SAFETY IN NUMBERS
A marine turtle lays up to 200
eggs, burying them in a nest in
the sand. If the nest remains
undiscovered, the eggs hatch
6 to 10 weeks later, but the
hatchlings fall prey to crabs,
seabirds, and other predators
on the way to the sea.

LIVE BIRTH
A rattlesnake keeps her
eggs inside her body
until they hatch, which
greatly improves their
chances of survival.
Approximately 10 to 20
young are born, measuring
about 13½ in (35 cm) in
length. The mother abandons
them soon after birth.

RATTLESNAKE AND YOUNG

More nests and eggs

Reptile eggs have shells that retain moisture so they can be laid on land. Most reptile eggs have soft, leathery shells, but some, such as a crocodile's, have hard shells. In most cases the eggs hatch outside the mother's body, although a few reptiles produce live young. In some cases the eggs hatch just before laying; in others, the embryos obtain nourishment from their mother through a placenta.

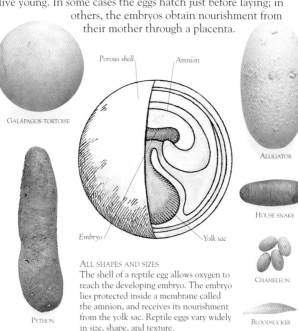

GALÁPAGOS TORTOISE

Porous shell

Amnion

Embryo

Yolk sac

ALLIGATOR

HOUSE SNAKE

CHAMELEON

PYTHON

BLOODSUCKER

ALL SHAPES AND SIZES

The shell of a reptile egg allows oxygen to reach the developing embryo. The embryo lies protected inside a membrane called the amnion, and receives its nourishment from the yolk sac. Reptile eggs vary widely in size, shape, and texture.

EGG TOOTH

As it grows inside the egg, a young lizard or snake develops a sharp "egg tooth" on the tip of its upper jaw. When the time for hatching arrives, the animal escapes from the shell by using the egg tooth to cut its way out.

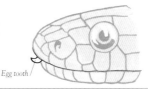

Egg tooth

HOW A SNAKE HATCHES

Just before a snake hatches, the yolk sac is drawn into the snake's body and the remaining yolk is absorbed into its intestine. Then, using its egg tooth, the snake cuts a slit large enough to push its head through. It may remain like this for up to two days before finally emerging from the egg. When it is fully hatched, the snake may be up to seven times longer than the egg from which it came.

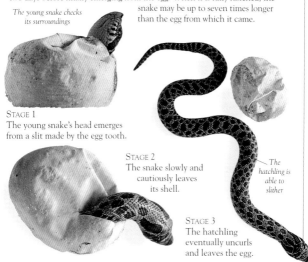

The young snake checks its surroundings

STAGE 1
The young snake's head emerges from a slit made by the egg tooth.

STAGE 2
The snake slowly and cautiously leaves its shell.

STAGE 3
The hatchling eventually uncurls and leaves the egg.

The hatchling is able to slither

DEADLY ENEMIES

MOST REPTILES are predators, but they are also preyed upon by other animals. Sometimes reptiles eat other reptiles. Eggs and young are especially vulnerable and in many cases adults, too, have their enemies. Even the largest and most dangerous reptiles may fall victim to human hunters.

A secretary bird either bites or tramples its reptile prey

SECRETARY BIRD
This African bird hunts tortoises, snakes, and lizards, flushing them from grass by stamping its feet. It uses its wings as a shield against venomous snakes.

The mongoose has lightning reactions

ENEMY FACTS
• When they are away from water, Nile crocodiles are vulnerable to attack by lions.
• The giant tortoises of Mauritius and Reunion Island were wiped out by hunters in the late 1700s.

Faced with a mongoose, a cobra looks fierce but its chances are slim

LEGENDARY ENEMIES
The mongoose is the only mammal that includes poisonous snakes in its diet. Although smaller than some of its prey, it is very courageous and is immune to snake venom. When tackling a snake, such as a spitting cobra, it bites the head of its prey with lightning speed.

SNAKE EATS SNAKE
Kingsnakes, some of which are also
known as milk snakes, feed on
small mammals, lizards,
frogs, and other snakes.
Kingsnakes, which
squeeze their prey, are
not afraid to tackle
venomous snakes,
such as copperheads.

Kingsnake

*A kingsnake
swallows a
copperhead*

| Copperhead

*A gull has easy
pickings when a
turtle nest
hatches*

HATCHLINGS AND GULL

GULL GAUNTLET
Young turtles hatch out from eggs buried
high on the beach. They immediately
head for the sea but, in doing so, run the
gauntlet of numerous predators. Seabirds,
such as gulls, gather in large numbers to
feast on the hatchlings, and many of them
never reach the safety of the water.

*The cobra
was pulled
out of a hole*

HUMAN HUNTERS
Humans hunt reptiles for
various reasons – for food,
for their skins, or simply
because they are poisonous.
Humans have also reduced
the natural habitat of many
species. A combination of
these factors has brought
some species to extinction
and made others very rare.

SOUTH INDIAN VILLAGERS DISPLAY A LIVE COBRA

BATTLE FOR SURVIVAL

SURVIVAL IN THE ANIMAL WORLD means not only being able to find something to eat but also avoiding being eaten by other animals. Large reptiles deter predators by their sheer size, but smaller species have to use a range of strategies, including camouflage, warning colours, mimicry, and bluff.

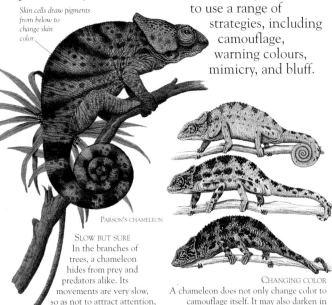

Skin cells draw pigments from below to change skin color

PARSON'S CHAMELEON

SLOW BUT SURE
In the branches of trees, a chameleon hides from prey and predators alike. Its movements are very slow, so as not to attract attention, and it adjusts its coloring to blend in with its surroundings.

CHANGING COLOR
A chameleon does not only change color to camouflage itself. It may also darken in heat or sunlight, or to indicate a change of mood – an angry chameleon turns black.

POISONOUS OR NOT?
The colorful warning stripes of a poisonous coral snake keep predators away. The harmless milk snake looks very much like a coral snake, with the result that predators avoid it, too.

SINOLOAN MILK SNAKE

HIDDEN SNAKE
The markings of a Gaboon viper camouflage it when it is lying among dead leaves. There, it can hide from prey when hunting – and also from potential predators.

Gaping mouth erects neck frill

Tail lashes to and fro

PURE BLUFF
When threatened, a frilled lizard opens its mouth wide, which spreads out the large frill of skin around its neck like an umbrella. At the same time it waves its legs, lashes its tail, and hisses in order to appear as fierce as possible.

Defense strategies

Reptiles have evolved many ways to avoid being eaten. Small lizards often use speed to escape, and many species retreat into underground burrows or rock crevices. Some use water as a means of escape. When cornered, many lizards, particularly large ones like monitors, will turn to face their attackers. Two lizards, the Gila monster and the beaded lizard, are venomous.

The snake lies absolutely still

The stinkpot is very aggressive

PLAYING DEAD
When it cannot escape, a grasss snake turns over, curls up, then lies still. It is playing dead, hoping its attacker will go away.

STINKING STINKPOT
The stinkpot turtle is the reptile equivalent of the skunk. It produces such an unpleasant smell that predators avoid it.

*As it loses speed, t|
basilisk drops into t|
water and must sw|*

BASILISK

SURVIVAL FACTS
• Horned lizards squirt blood at their attackers from their eyes.
• Some skinks have a bright blue tail that attracts predators away from vital body parts.

LOSING A TAIL TO SAVE A LIFE
In many cases a lizard can shed its tail if it is grabbed by an attacker. The tail is equipped with special breaking points in the vertebrae, and the shed tail usually twitches for a while after it breaks off, distracting the attacker long enough for the lizard to make good its escape. A new tail grows.

Tail recently shed

New tail after eight months

Growing the new tail uses up energy

TREE SKINK

Tail can only break in the old part, where there are still breakable vertebrae

Tail helps basilisk balance as it runs

RUNNING ON WATER
Basilisks have long hind legs for running, and their feet have broad soles with a fringe of scales around the toes. This enables them to run across water in order to escape from potential predators.

LIVING IN WATER

ALTHOUGH REPTILES EVOLVED as land animals, many species have become adapted to living in water, where food is often plentiful. For these species, swimming is more important than walking, and many are equipped with paddles instead of feet. But they are still air-breathing animals and so have special adaptations enabling them to cope with a watery environment.

GOGGLE EYES
Crocodilians, like this caiman, lie submerged in the water, waiting for prey. The eyes and nostrils are placed high on the head so that only these parts show above the water.

The spectacled caiman has a bony ridge between its eyes, resembling the frame of a pair of glasses

SNORKELING TURTLE

The matamata turtle of Brazil waits for its prey on the river bed. It pokes its nostrils out of the water to breathe, without moving – thus it avoids disturbing the fish.

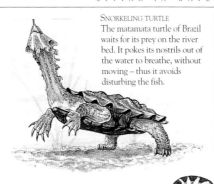

WATER FACTS

• Sea turtles excrete salt absorbed in sea water from their eyes, which is why they seem to cry.

• To prevent water from getting into its lung, a sea snake closes off its nostrils with a spongelike tissue.

Sea snakes are very poisonous

Powerful tail moves the snake forward

PADDLE TAIL

A sea snake is virtually helpless on land but is an excellent swimmer. Its tail is flattened vertically to form a powerful, oarlike paddle.

The four paddles propel the turtle

WEB-FOOTED SLIDER

Freshwater chelonians, such as terrapins, have webbed feet for swimming. The red-eared slider has a habit of sliding back into the water if disturbed.

PADDLE FEET

A marine turtle can tolerate high levels of carbon dioxide in its blood and so can swim under water for long periods.

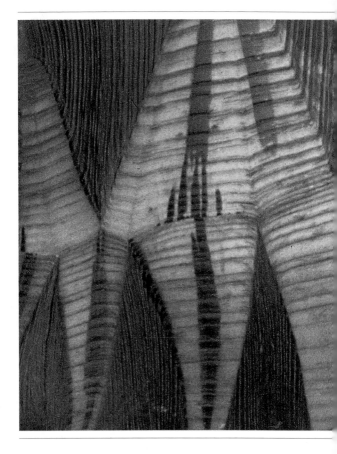

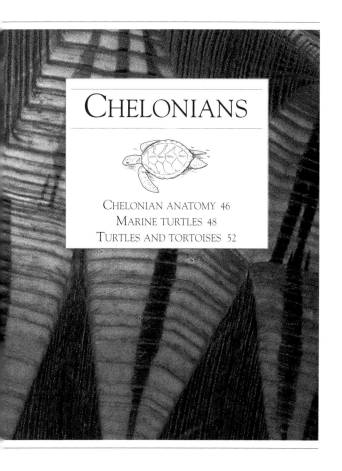

CHELONIANS

CHELONIAN ANATOMY

CHELONIANS are reptiles whose bodies are protected by shells. The shells are made up of the plastron which protects the belly, and the carapace, which covers the back. There are between 250 and 300 species of chelonian. Some live in salt water, others in fresh water, and yet others on land. Water dwellers are usually called turtles or terrapins, while land dwellers are known as tortoises.

Carapace

FROM THE OUTSIDE
The red-eared terrapin is a typical chelonian. It has a carapace made up of several layers. The outer layer consists of horny shields, known as scutes.

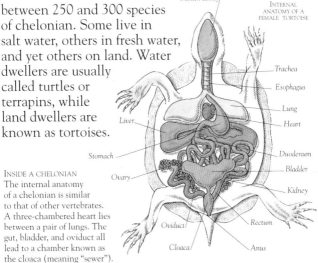

INTERNAL ANATOMY OF A FEMALE TORTOISE

Mouth cavity
Trachea
Esophagus
Lung
Heart
Liver
Duodenum
Stomach
Bladder
Ovary
Kidney
Oviduct
Rectum
Cloaca
Anus

INSIDE A CHELONIAN
The internal anatomy of a chelonian is similar to that of other vertebrates. A three-chambered heart lies between a pair of lungs. The gut, bladder, and oviduct all lead to a chamber known as the cloaca (meaning "sewer").

FUSED VERTEBRAE

The carapace is made up of about 50 bony plates formed in the skin. The shell has an outer layer of horny shields and an inner one of bone. The vertebrae, with the ribs and the two limb girdles, are fused to the carapace. This has resulted in the limb girdles being inside the ribs.

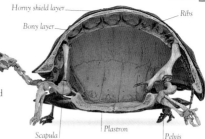

Horny shield layer

Bony layer

Ribs

Scapula

Plastron

Pelvis

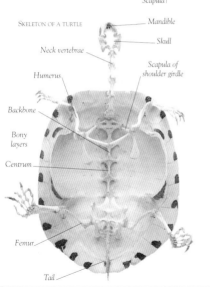

SKELETON OF A TURTLE

Mandible

Skull

Neck vertebrae

Scapula of shoulder girdle

Humerus

Backbone

Bony layers

Centrum

Femur

Tail

FLEXIBLE NECK

Inside the horny outer layer, the carapace is made of several layers of bone. The eight neck vertebrae are very flexible. The upper limb bones are short, with enlarged ends to take the weight of the animal's body and shell.

CHELONIAN FACTS

• Some female turtles produce eggs four years after mating.

• All chelonians lay eggs on land, even the marine turtles.

• Some turtles can live for more than a year without food.

MARINE TURTLES

TURTLES INVADED the world's seas and oceans during the Triassic period, some 200 million years ago. Today there are seven species, six of which are grouped together in the one family, the Chelonidae. The leatherback turtle is classified by itself in another family, called the Dermochelidae.

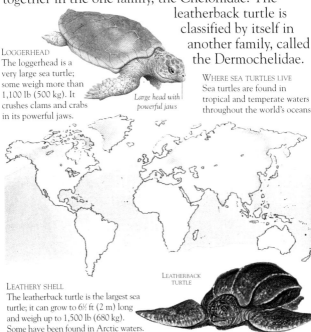

LOGGERHEAD
The loggerhead is a very large sea turtle; some weigh more than 1,100 lb (500 kg). It crushes clams and crabs in its powerful jaws.

Large head with powerful jaws

WHERE SEA TURTLES LIVE
Sea turtles are found in tropical and temperate waters throughout the world's oceans

LEATHERBACK TURTLE

LEATHERY SHELL
The leatherback turtle is the largest sea turtle; it can grow to 6½ ft (2 m) long and weigh up to 1,500 lb (680 kg). Some have been found in Arctic waters.

IMMUNE TO POISON
Hawksbill turtles are found near coral reefs. They feed on invertebrates, such as sponges, many of which contain poisons. These do not affect the turtles but may kill animals that eat them.

NESTING TOGETHER
Ridley turtles come ashore in large numbers to nest together on certain beaches. Each female digs a hole in which she lays about 100 eggs. Olive ridleys live in the Atlantic, Indian, and parts of the Pacific Oceans.

CHELONIAN FEET

The limbs of marine turtles are very different from those of land and freshwater chelonians. Land tortoises have large, clawed feet. Freshwater turtles have webbing between the toes. Marine turtles have no claws; instead, their limbs have evolved into flippers.

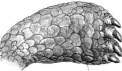

LAND TORTOISE

Clawed foot for crawling on land

MARINE TURTLE

Flipper used for swimming

FRESHWATER TURTLE

Turtles in danger

Sea turtles are among the world's most vulnerable animals. They are relatively slow moving and easy to catch, and their nest sites are mostly well known – for example, Kemp's ridley turtles only nest on one beach in Mexico. Turtle products are much in demand, and large numbers of turtles are killed. In addition, their overall rate of reproduction is slow; although a green turtle may lay 1,000 eggs in one season, only a few survive into adulthood.

TURTLE EXPLOITATION

Turtles are large, meaty animals and in many places are hunted for food; green turtles are especially prized, particularly for turtle soup. When polished, the shell of a green turtle is a popular tourist souvenir. Pieces of turtle shell are also used in furniture-making.

GREEN TURTLE EGGS

END OF THE LINE
Green turtle eggs are a popular food. The nests are easy to find since the females leave an obvious trail to the nest.

TURTLES FOR SALE
Rows of stuffed turtles provide an income for a local trader. Trade in wild turtles is banned under the provisions of international agreements on trade in endangered animal products. Some trade in specially bred animals is allowed.

STUFFED TURTLES

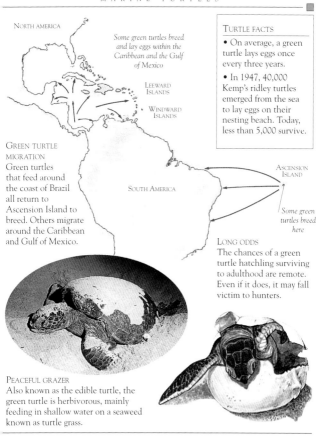

NORTH AMERICA

Some green turtles breed and lay eggs within the Caribbean and the Gulf of Mexico

LEEWARD ISLANDS

WINDWARD ISLANDS

TURTLE FACTS

• On average, a green turtle lays eggs once every three years.

• In 1947, 40,000 Kemp's ridley turtles emerged from the sea to lay eggs on their nesting beach. Today, less than 5,000 survive.

GREEN TURTLE MIGRATION
Green turtles that feed around the coast of Brazil all return to Ascension Island to breed. Others migrate around the Caribbean and Gulf of Mexico.

SOUTH AMERICA

ASCENSION ISLAND

Some green turtles breed here

LONG ODDS
The chances of a green turtle hatchling surviving to adulthood are remote. Even if it does, it may fall victim to hunters.

PEACEFUL GRAZER
Also known as the edible turtle, the green turtle is herbivorous, mainly feeding in shallow water on a seaweed known as turtle grass.

TURTLES AND TORTOISES

THE ORIGINS of the first chelonians are obscure because there is very little fossil evidence. However, it seems likely that their ancestors belonged to an early group of reptiles known as diadectomorphs that lived in swamplands. As some of them moved farther onto the land, they acquired protective shells. Some ancestors of modern chelonians remained on land; others returned to the water.

Soft shell

Snorkel-like nose for breathing when underwater

SOFT KILLER

The shell of a soft-shelled turtle is covered in leathery skin instead of horny plates. Soft-shelled turtles are found in southern Asia, Africa, and North America. They live in rivers where they feed on water creatures, striking with lightning speed.

Fish being sucked in

FISH SUCKER

Disguised as a rock, the matamata turtle of South America lurks on the river bed patiently waiting for a fish to swim close by. When its prey approaches, it expands its throat and sucks the fish into its gaping mouth.

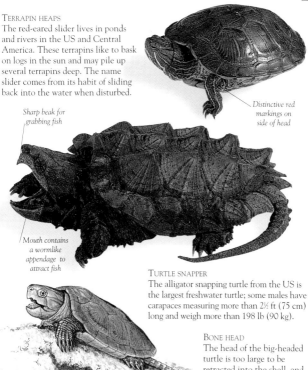

TERRAPIN HEAPS
The red-eared slider lives in ponds
and rivers in the US and Central
America. These terrapins like to bask
on logs in the sun and may pile up
several terrapins deep. The name
slider comes from its habit of sliding
back into the water when disturbed.

*Sharp beak for
grabbing fish*

*Distinctive red
markings on
side of head*

*Mouth contains
a wormlike
appendage to
attract fish*

TURTLE SNAPPER
The alligator snapping turtle from the US is
the largest freshwater turtle; some males have
carapaces measuring more than 2½ ft (75 cm)
long and weigh more than 198 lb (90 kg).

BONE HEAD
The head of the big-headed
turtle is too large to be
retracted into the shell, and
so it has a bony roof with a
tough outer scute. A skillful
climber, this turtle may feed
away from water.

BIG-HEADED TURTLE

More chelonians

Tortoises are among the most popular reptiles, being slow-moving, peaceful herbivores. Species of tortoise that have evolved in isolated places, where predators are few and competition for food is slight, may live to great ages and grow to vast sizes. Freshwater turtles are carnivorous and tend to be much more active.

RED-LEGGED TORTOISE

RED FEET
The red-legged tortoise is common in South America where it lives in rainforests. Large specimens can reach 19½ in (50 cm) in length.

PANCAKE TORTOISES
An African pancake tortoise's shell is light and flattened in shape, enabling it to move quickly and climb over rocks. It can also squeeze into small spaces when danger threatens.

PANCAKE TORTOISE

HINGE-BACK
The hinge-back tortoises of southern Africa have a hinge of cartilaginous tissue that allows the back of the shell to drop and protect the animal's rear. Hinge-backs sometimes share their burrow with lizards.

STARRED CAMOUFLAGE

The starred tortoise is found in India and Sri Lanka. It is well camouflaged; its shell blends in with dry grassland. Less than 9½ in (25 cm) long, it crawls slowly, at little over ⅛ mph (0.2 km/h).

STARRED TORTOISE

Sturdy legs

Shell may be up to a foot (30 cm) long

SNAKE-NECK

The snake-necked turtles of Australia live in rivers, where they hunt freshwater animals. However, like all chelonians, they leave the water to lay eggs in a nest on dry land. When threatened, they fold the head back into the shell.

Neck is nearly as long as the shell

SNAKE-NECKED TURTLE

GALÁPAGOS TORTOISE

GALÁPAGOS GIANT

The lumbering giant tortoises of the Galápagos Islands weigh up to 198 lb (90 kg). They were originally present in large numbers, but predation by humans, dogs, and pigs, plus competition for food with goats, have brought about a severe decline in numbers.

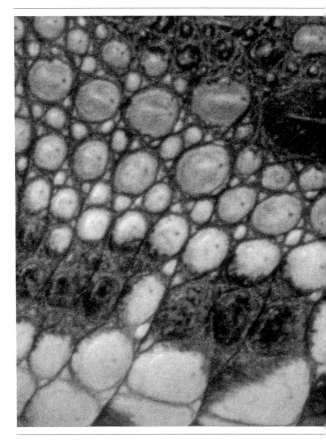

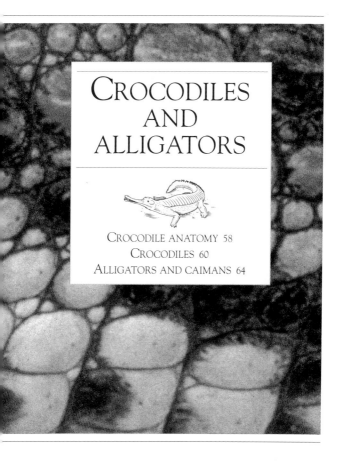

CROCODILES AND ALLIGATORS

CROCODILE ANATOMY

CROCODILES AND ALLIGATORS are the only remaining group of archosaurs, or "ruling reptiles" – the group to which the dinosaurs belonged. They are large animals with an armored skin that covers the whole body. Apart from the estuarine crocodile, they are found near the shores of freshwater rivers and lakes in warm regions of the world.

CROCODILE-
BONE
FIGURINE

CROCODILE BONE
Animal bones have often been used to make ornaments. This Egyptian figurine was carved from a crocodile bone.

NILE CROCODILE
The Nile crocodile is found in many parts of Africa, although its range has been much reduced due to hunting. It often swims out to sea, and so is also found in Madagascar.

Powerful tail

ANATOMY FACTS

• A crocodile's skin is composed of partly ossified (converted into bone) horny plates.

• Crocodilians propel themselves through the water with their powerful tail.

SKELETON
Like all crocodilians, a caiman has a long skull, with nostrils and eyes set high. The body is long with two pairs of short legs held out sideways from the body.

Hind feet with
four toes

Tail vertebrae

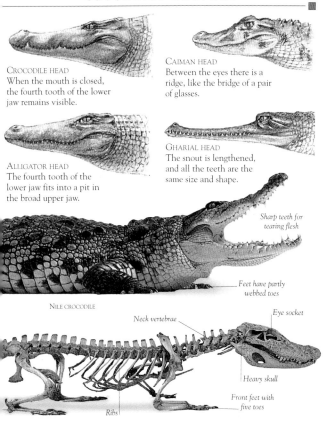

CROCODILE HEAD
When the mouth is closed,
the fourth tooth of the lower
jaw remains visible.

CAIMAN HEAD
Between the eyes there is a
ridge, like the bridge of a pair
of glasses.

ALLIGATOR HEAD
The fourth tooth of the
lower jaw fits into a pit in
the broad upper jaw.

GHARIAL HEAD
The snout is lengthened,
and all the teeth are the
same size and shape.

Sharp teeth for tearing flesh

Feet have partly webbed toes

NILE CROCODILE

Neck vertebrae

Eye socket

Heavy skull

Front feet with five toes

Ribs

CROCODILES

CROCODILES ARE FOUND in many tropical parts of the world. Large species include the American crocodile, the Orinoco crocodile, the Nile crocodile, and the saltwater crocodile, all of which can grow to more than 23 ft (7 m) in length. Smaller species include the mugger of India and Sri Lanka, and the Australian crocodile.

Prominent tooth

SKULL
A crocodile's skull is almost solid bone. The jaws are long, for holding prey, but the teeth cannot slice or chew, only tear.

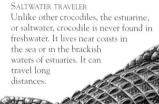

SALTWATER TRAVELER
Unlike other crocodiles, the estuarine, or saltwater, crocodile is never found in freshwater. It lives near coasts in the sea or in the brackish waters of estuaries. It can travel long distances.

Eye socket

CROCODILE SKULL
(TOP VIEW)

Female guards young in mouth

SHARING A MEAL
In Africa, crocodiles feed mostly on antelopes, which are seized as they come near the water to drink. However, other animals are also taken, and crocodiles will feed on animals that have died, such as this zebra.

LYING IN WAIT
Even large animals, such as wildebeest, may fall victim to a crocodile attack. With a sudden rush, the crocodile grabs the prey in its jaws and drags it into the water to drown.

UNLIKELY PARTNERS
As a crocodile lies with its mouth open, to keep cool, a spur-winged plover picks food from between its teeth. This looks dangerous for the bird, but the crocodile may benefit from having its teeth cleaned and the plover's cry warns the crocodile of danger.

ESTUARINE
CROCODILE

Crocodiles

An adult crocodile swallows stones, which accumulate in its stomach. The stones do not break up food, but scientists believe that they may act as ballast, allowing the animal to remain submerged under the water.

CROCODILE SKIN

NILE CROCODILE

CRACKING EGGS
When her eggs are about to hatch, the female uncovers them. She may gently crack them to help the young emerge.

SHOES AND HANDBAGS
Formerly many wild crocodiles and alligators were hunted for their skins, used for making shoes, handbags, and suitcases. Wild crocodiles are now protected, but are still illegally killed.

CROCODILE FACTS

• A saltwater crocodile arrived at the Cocos Islands in the Indian Ocean, having swum 684 miles (1,100 km).

• The ancient Egyptians worshiped a crocodile-headed god named Sebek.

ESTUARINE CROCODILE

CROCODILE TEARS
The estuarine crocodile gets rid of the excess salt it swallows with its food by excreting it via the tear glands in its eyes.

THE GHARIAL

The family Gavialidae contains just one species, the gharial, or Indian gavial. The Gavialidae is thought to have arisen during the Cretaceous period, some 100 million years ago. The modern gharial has rather weak limbs and spends nearly all its life in water, using its oar-like tail for swimming. It lives in the deep waters of the Ganges, Mahanadi, and Brahmaputra Rivers of India, as well as the Koladan and Maingtha Rivers in Southeast Asia.

GHARIAL SKULL
(TOP VIEW)

Holes allow space for jaw muscles to expand when feeding

Eye socket

NO PROTECTION
For a long time, the gharial was protected from hunters because it was sacred to the Hindu god Vishnu. Today, however, it is illegally hunted for its skin.

FISH FEEDER
The gharial feeds entirely on fish. It lies in wait, moving its head from side to side to cover a large area, and catches its prey with a sudden jerk of its head.

LONG SNOUT
The main characteristic of the gharial is its long snout. At the tip it widens into an oval area that bears the nostrils; in males this region is bulbous. Each jaw contains more than 50 sharp teeth.

Nasal opening

ALLIGATORS AND CAIMANS

ALLIGATORS AND CAIMANS have shorter snouts than crocodiles, and they live solely in freshwater. There are two species of alligator, the American alligator and the rare Chinese alligator. The various species of caiman are all found in the Americas, ranging from Mexico to South America and the Caribbean.

SLOW DOWN, LIVE LONGER
Alligators are more sluggish than crocodiles. This may be why they live longer – there are records of alligators living for up to 50 years. Widespread hunting, however, severely threatens the animal's survival in the wild.

AMERICAN ALLIGATOR

Males roar during breeding season

SKULL
An alligator's skull is shorter and broader than a crocodile's. The fearsome jaws can carry young with surprising delicacy.

HUNTED DOWN
American alligators can grow to 20 ft (6 m) in length, but because of hunting it is rare nowadays to find individuals longer than 10 ft (3 m).

CAIMAN

The skin on a caiman's belly is reinforced with bony plates, making it difficult for use as leather. Caimans are still hunted – to protect livestock.

Caimans can move surprisingly quickly on land

Hind foot is used to scratch body, rub eyes, and tear food

Caimans hiss when threatened

YOUNG ALLIGATORS

ALLIGATOR YOUNG

Alligators are 8 in (20 cm) long at hatching. They grow 1 ft (30 cm) each year, reaching maturity at six. The young are vulnerable to predators, including mammals, birds, and fish, and, at any stage, may be eaten by other alligators.

Adults feed on fish and small mammals

ALLIGATOR FACTS

• The English word "alligator" comes from the Spanish for lizard, *largato*.

• The Chinese alligator is nearly extinct. It is killed for food and to make charms and medicines.

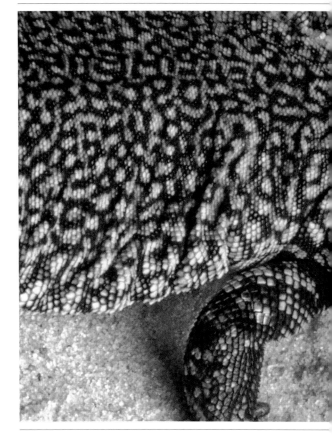

LIZARDS

LIZARD ANATOMY

THE FIRST LIZARDS appeared 200 million years ago, in the Triassic period. They fed on insects and looked similar to modern lizards. Typically, a lizard has a broad head, a long, slender body with limbs held out sideways, and a long tail. However, there are more specialized forms, such as chameleons and legless lizards.

ANATOMY OF A FEMALE LIZARD

Heart

Ovary

Lungs

Intestine

Opening of cloaca

INTERNAL ANATOMY
A lizard's body is symmetrically arranged both externally and internally. As in nearly all reptiles, the heart has three chambers and the gut, oviduct, and ureter empty into a common chamber, the cloaca.

UNUSUAL LIZARD
A chameleon does not have the flexible spine of most lizards. In addition, its legs are proportionately longer, and it can raise its body higher than other lizards.

Spine is less flexible than other lizards'

Prehensile tail for gripping onto branches

CHAMELEON SKELETON

Broad body with many ribs

Toes designed for grasping

GLASS LIZARD
A glass lizard can easily be mistaken for a snake, but is in fact a lizard that has lost its front legs and retained only the tiny remnants of hind legs. This is an adaptation for burrowing underground.

A glass lizard can easily hide under a stone or log

LIZARD FACTS
• Only two lizards have a poisonous bite, the beaded lizard and its close relative, the Gila monster.

• Some lizards, particularly whiptail lizards, can lay fertile eggs without mating.

ORIENTAL LONG-TAILED LIZARD
The Oriental long-tailed lizard lives in grassy places from China to Sumatra. The tail, which is three to five times as long as the rest of the body, spreads the lizard's weight over a number of grass stems. This allows the lizard to run easily across the softest grass.

Brille

EYE CLEANING
A gecko does not have movable eyelids. Instead, each of its eyes is covered by a transparent scale, known as a brille. It keeps this clean by licking it.

MADAGASCAR DAY GECKO

HOW LIZARDS FEED

SOME LIZARDS eat almost anything; others, such as the plant-eating Galápagos iguanas, have a specialized diet. Many lizards prey on insects, and some of them also eat vegetable matter. Some species prey on other animals, such as birds, small mammals, and other lizards.

VEGETARIAN
The Galápagos land iguana feeds only on plants, particularly the fleshy leaves and fruits of the prickly pear cactus. It deals with the spines by working the food around in its mouth until they break off.

GALÁPAGOS LAND IGUANA

CHAMELEON

Insect trapped in sticky mucus

Muscular tongue is as long as the lizard's body

STICKY TONGUE
A chameleon moves very slowly and deliberately toward its potential prey. When within range, it shoots out its long, muscular tongue at incredible speed. The insect is trapped on the end of the lizard's sticky tongue and drawn into its mouth.

EYED LIZARD

CATCHING INSECTS

The eyed lizard feeds on insects, small birds, rodents, and some fruits. An insect, such as a cricket, is shaken rapidly to stun it and then passed to the back of the lizard's mouth. It is then crushed by the jaws in a series of rapid, powerful snaps.

The eyed or jeweled lizard is native to southern Europe and North Africa

ANT EATER

Despite its fierce appearance, the Australian thorny devil, or moloch, lives solely on ants, which it eats in large quantities. It obtains much of its water from dew, which condenses on its spines and runs into its mouth.

THORNY DEVIL

KOMODO DRAGON

PREDATORY DRAGON

The huge Komodo dragon is a large monitor lizard found only on a few Indonesian islands, including Komodo. It feeds mostly on carrion, but is capable of catching and killing a small deer.

FEEDING FACTS

• The caiman lizards of South America feed almost exclusively on marsh snails.

• In crowded conditions, chameleons have been known to eat the young of their own species.

THE WORLD'S LIZARDS

BECAUSE THEY ARE COLD-BLOODED and use their environment to maintain body temperature, lizards prefer warm climates. Thus most species are found in tropical and subtropical regions. There are 14 families, the largest of which are the skinks (about 1000 species), the geckos (830 species), the iguanids (650 species), and the agamids (300 species).

Large toes with hooked pads

GECKO

MARINE IGUANA

BY THE SEA
The Galápagos marine iguana can often be seen sunning itself on seashore rocks. It feeds solely on seaweed and is an excellent swimmer.

HOUSE GUEST
Pads on the gecko's feet help it cling to any surface. Geckos can often be seen hunting for insects on walls in the tropics.

LIZARD FACTS

• Some lizards, such as the common lizard and slow worm of Britain, do live in temperate climates.

• On West Indian islands, numbers of anoles (which belong to the iguanids) exceed 20,000 per acre.

MADAGASCAR
DAY GECKO

FOREST DWELLER
This gecko's bright green coloration is perfect camouflage for its home – the forests of Madagascar. Unlike most geckos, it hunts during the day.

IN THE JUNGLE
Some rain forest iguanas are
slender animals with long toes.
Males are often larger and
more brightly colored than
females. In some species,
the colors become
more apparent
during the
breeding season.

PLUMED BASILISK
The most spectacular
species of basilisk is the
Central and South American
plumed basilisk, which has a
sail-like crest along its head and
back. The male displays its crest
during the breeding season.

PLUMED BASILISK

Long hind legs

ON WATER
Basilisks are found in
Central and South
America, near streams and
lakes. Their splayed feet and long
tails enable them to run across the
surface of the water.

DESERT ISLANDER
The common, or
green, iguana is
found in Central
and South
America and on many
Caribbean islands.
There are about
650 species of iguana.

COMMON IGUANA

The Agamid family

Agamids, of which there are about 300 species, are found in central, south, and Southeast Asia, Australia, and Africa. The only species found in Europe is the starred lizard, or hardun, which lives on some Greek islands, in North Africa, and in southwest Asia. Many species spend their lives in the branches of trees, but agamids have adapted to a wide range of habitats. Some species live at high altitudes; *Agama himalayama* is found on Himalayan slopes at 11,000 ft (3,300 m).

GARDEN LIZARD

BLOODSUCKER
Like a chameleon, the garden lizard, or bloodsucker, can change color rapidly. It is found in India, Afghanistan, and China.

Large scales protect underside of jaw

BEARDED
DRAGON
Some seven species of Australian lizard are known as bearded dragons because of the long, pointed scales on their throats.

BEARDED DRAGON

THORNY DEVIL

Spines provide excellent defense

HOT AND SPINY
The thorny devil, or moloch, is an Australian desert dweller. It allows its body to heat up to an almost lethal temperature so that it can spend as much time as possible feeding in the open.

SPINY TAIL
Spring-tailed lizards tolerate very high temperatures and are among the hardiest lizards of the African Sahara. They feed on plants and insects and survive on the moisture they obtain from their food and from dew.

Channels between scales guide water condensed from the air toward the mouth

SPRING-TAILED LIZARD

"Eyebrows" protect eyes from twigs and leaves

Spiny tail is used for defense and acts as a fat store

Dorsal crest of pointed scales

PRICKLY NECK
The pricklenape agama lives high in the trees in mountain forests from China to Indonesia. Its name comes from the long, sharp spines on its neck. Its long toes have fringed scales that help it cling to branches.

PRICKLENAPE AGAMA

WATER DRAGON
The crested water dragon is an Asian species. It lives mainly in trees that grow near water. If disturbed on the ground, it escapes by rearing up on its hind legs and running off in a burst of speed.

CRESTED WATER DRAGON

Tail acts as balance when runing

More lizards of the world

Many lizards are specially adapted for particular environments.
A chameleon's body, for example, is greatly modified for living in
trees. The body is flattened from side to
side, a shape that helps the reptile
avoid the heat of the sun during the
hottest part of the day, but absorb
heat in the early morning and
late evening. It also helps to
camouflage the body and
makes it easier to balance
on the branches of trees.

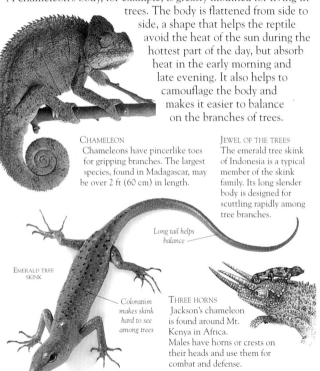

CHAMELEON
Chameleons have pincerlike toes
for gripping branches. The largest
species, found in Madagascar, may
be over 2 ft (60 cm) in length.

JEWEL OF THE TREES
The emerald tree skink
of Indonesia is a typical
member of the skink
family. Its long slender
body is designed for
scuttling rapidly among
tree branches.

Long tail helps
balance

EMERALD TREE
SKINK

Coloration
makes skink
hard to see
among trees

THREE HORNS
Jackson's chameleon
is found around Mt.
Kenya in Africa.
Males have horns or crests on
their heads and use them for
combat and defense.

WHIPTAIL

Most whiptails have long stripes

WHIPTAIL
Whiptails are slender, agile lizards that are found in a variety of habitats from southern North America southward to Argentina. This species lives in dry grasslands.

Long toes assist grip

SKINK IN DANGER
The giant skink of the Solomon Islands grows to more than 2 ft (70 cm) and is the largest of the family. It lives in trees, feeding on leaves. Like many reptiles, it is threatened by the destruction of its habitat. It is also hunted for food.

Large, overlapping scales

Head-shaped tail

STUMP-TAILED SKINK

TWO HEADS
Southern Australia's stump-tailed skink (also known as the shingleback or pinecone lizard) has a tail that looks almost exactly like its head. This often confuses predators long enough for it to escape.

GIANT SKINK

Lizard protection

For a small animal that lives in the open, a scaly skin affords only limited protection, and so some lizards have additional protective features. Girdle-tailed lizards and their relatives are well armored, and the armadillo lizard makes good defensive use of its spines. Beaded lizards, such as the Gila monster, defend themselves with poison, while monitor lizards are protected by their sheer size.

Hissing warns off an attacker

ON GUARD
Gould's monitor uses its tail as a third hind leg to threaten an attacker or simply raise itself up and survey its surroundings. Monitors include a number of large lizards, and 20 of the 30 known species are Australian.

GOULD'S MONITOR

Thick scales protect body

Male is brightly colored during the breeding season

Food consists mostly of insects, with some plant material

Female lays a few eggs in a communal nesting site

FLAT LIZARD

STUCK FAST
The flat lizards of southern Africa live in rock crevices. When threatened, a flat lizard inflates its body, jamming it into a crevice and making it impossible for a predator to prize out.

ARMOR PLATING

The plated lizards of Africa have an armored covering of large rectangular scales arranged in rows down the body. The body is thus fairly rigid, and to allow for expansion after a meal, there is a deep pleat of skin that runs from the angle of the jaw to the hind limbs.

Thick scales protect body

Food consists of both insects and plants

Inward fold of skin

Belly protected by spiky head and tail

BALL OF PRICKLES

The African armadillo lizard has an unusual method of defense, reminiscent of that of an armadillo. It curls itself up and grasps its tail in its mouth, presenting an attacker with a prickly problem.

Body is about 1 ft (30 cm) long but only ½ in (1 cm) thick

GILA MONSTER

The Gila (pronounced "heela") monster of the southwestern US is one of only two poisonous lizards. Its venom glands discharge into its mouth near large, grooved fangs. The venom is not injected, but seeps in when the lizard bites.

Pink and black coloration warns reptile is poisonous

THE TUATARA

THE TUATARA LOOKS LIKE A LIZARD, but it differs from true lizards in the structure of its skeleton and skull. In fact, it is the sole survivor of the rynchocephalians, a primitive reptile group that thrived between 100 and 200 million years ago, during the Jurassic and Triassic periods.

"Tuatara" is Maori for "peaks on the back"

LIVING FOSSIL
The tuatara is called a living fossil because it has changed little in 200 million years. All its closest relatives died out; no one knows why the tuatara alone survived.

LONG LIFE
Male tuataras grow to about 2 ft (61 cm) long; females are slightly shorter. Both sexes reach sexual maturity at the age of 20, and may live for another 100 years.

LIZARD ANCESTORS
Homoeosaurus, a relative of the tuatara, lived about 140 million years ago. Its ancestors probably evolved from lizards 200 million years ago.

MALE TUATARA

Short, powerful legs for burrowing

A third, or pineal, eye under the skin may act as a thermostat or help to regulate the tuatara's "biological clock"

Crest runs down the back and tail

FEMALE TUATARA

A LONG WAIT
After mating, a female tuatara stores the male's sperm for 10–12 months before fertilization occurs. She then lays 5–15 eggs in a shallow burrow.

SKULL STRUCTURE
The tuatara's skull is different from that of lizards. It resembles a crocodile's in having two bony arches at the back. Most lizards have just one arch, while in burrowing lizards and snakes the arches have disappeared.

Teeth are fused with the jaws

Two bony arches

Tuatara has large, wedge-shaped teeth at the front

TUATARA SKULL

ISLAND HOME
Tuataras are found on a few small islands off the coast of New Zealand. They live in burrows (which they often share with seabirds) and are active at night, when they come out to search for insects and earthworms. They grow very slowly.

TUATARA FACTS
• Eggs hatch 15 months after laying – the longest incubation period of any reptile.

• A tuatara breathes very slowly, about once every seven seconds, and can hold its breath for nearly an hour.

SNAKES

SNAKE ANATOMY

SNAKES ARE PROBABLY descended from burrowing lizards that gradually lost their legs as they adapted to an underground life. Today's snakes do not generally live underground, but they have retained their ancestral form and found new ways of getting around.

RHINOCEROS VIPER

VENOMOUS RHINO
Like all snakes, the deadly African rhinoceros viper has a long, legless body. Its name comes from the rhino-like "horns" (actually long scales) on its nose.

INSIDE A SNAKE
A snake's body is long and thin, so the stomach, liver, kidneys, and ovaries are greatly elongated, as is the right lung; the left lung is very small. The intestines form a long tube straight down the body.

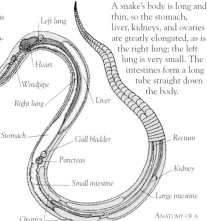

Left lung

Heart

Windpipe

Right lung

Liver

Stomach

Gall bladder

Rectum

Pancreas

Kidney

Small intestine

Large intestine

Ovaries

ANATOMY OF A FEMALE SNAKE

SNAKE FACTS
• The longest snakes have skeletons with some 400 vertebrae.

• Snakes can probably hear only a limited range of sounds.

• Some snakes use part of the windpipe as an extra lung.

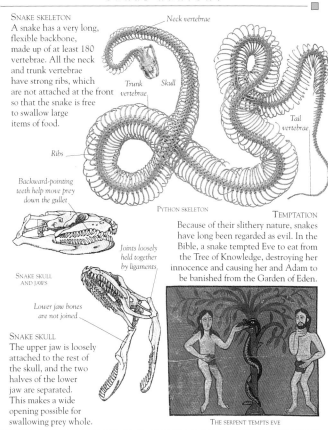

SNAKE SKELETON
A snake has a very long, flexible backbone, made up of at least 180 vertebrae. All the neck and trunk vertebrae have strong ribs, which are not attached at the front so that the snake is free to swallow large items of food.

Neck vertebrae

Trunk vertebrae

Skull

Tail vertebrae

Ribs

PYTHON SKELETON

Backward-pointing teeth help move prey down the gullet

SNAKE SKULL AND JAWS

Joints loosely held together by ligaments

Lower jaw bones are not joined

SNAKE SKULL
The upper jaw is loosely attached to the rest of the skull, and the two halves of the lower jaw are separated. This makes a wide opening possible for swallowing prey whole.

TEMPTATION
Because of their slithery nature, snakes have long been regarded as evil. In the Bible, a snake tempted Eve to eat from the Tree of Knowledge, destroying her innocence and causing her and Adam to be banished from the Garden of Eden.

THE SERPENT TEMPTS EVE

CONSTRICTORS

BOAS, PYTHONS, AND ANACONDAS are known as constrictors – snakes that kill by wrapping prey in their strong body coils until the animal suffocates. Their victims are usually mammals, but many constrictors kill birds as well, and some are known to prey on other reptiles.

Coils tighten each time the rat breathes out

BALL PYTHON

DEADLY SQUEEZE
This West African ball python is killing its prey, a rat, by coiling itself around the animal's chest and gradually tightening its grip. Soon, the rat will not be able to inhale, and it will die from suffocation.

BIRDS BEWARE
Tree boas hunt birds by creeping up on them as they roost in the branches of trees; mammals are also eaten. The emerald tree boa lives in the lush rain forests of the Amazon basin.

EMERALD TREE BOA

PRIMITIVE SNAKES
Scientists call pythons,
boas, and some other species
"primitive" because these
snakes have tiny claws where
the hind legs and hips of
their lizard ancestors once
were. The claws lie on either
side of the cloaca and are
said to play a part in mating.

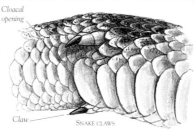

Cloacal opening

Claw

SNAKE CLAWS

HOW A CONSTRICTOR CONSUMES ITS PREY

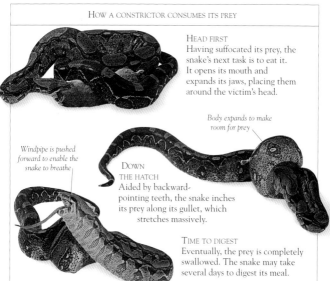

HEAD FIRST
Having suffocated its prey, the
snake's next task is to eat it.
It opens its mouth and
expands its jaws, placing them
around the victim's head.

Body expands to make room for prey

Windpipe is pushed forward to enable the snake to breathe

DOWN
THE HATCH
Aided by backward-
pointing teeth, the snake inches
its prey along its gullet, which
stretches massively.

TIME TO DIGEST
Eventually, the prey is completely
swallowed. The snake may take
several days to digest its meal.

Boas

All but three species of boa are found in the
tropical warmth of Central and South America.
These constrictors have adapted to a wide
variety of habitats, many spending their lives
in trees, while a number of others live on
the ground or burrow into it.

COOK'S TREE
BOA

RAINBOW COLORS
The dazzlingly
iridescent rainbow
boa lives in the forests,
woodlands, and
grassy plains of
northwestern
South America.
It feeds on small
mammals and birds.

RAINBOW BOA

BOA CONSTRICTOR
The red-tailed boa
is one of 11
subspecies of boa
constrictor. It grows
to an average of 10 ft
(3 m) in length
(although snakes over
13 ft [4 m] have been
seen), and lives in the
semidesert plains of
northwestern Peru.

RED-TAILED BOA

COOK'S BOA
Cook's tree boa is the largest
of several subspecies of tree
or garden boa. It is found
only on the Caribbean
islands of Trinidad,
Grenada, Carriacou,
Union, and St. Vincent.

PACIFIC BOA

BOA FACTS

• When a rubber boa is threatened, it rolls itself into a ball, hides its head among its coils, and presents its tail toward the intruder.

• Boas do not hatch from eggs. Instead, females give birth to live young.

CUNNING IMPOSTER

The Pacific boa, native to the rain forests, marshes, and swamps of New Guinea and nearby islands, lives and hunts on the ground. To defend itself against attack, it mimics a venomous viper, hissing and striking at the intruder.

TREE OR GARDEN BOA

AGILE TREE DWELLER

The tree boa of northern South America and southern Central America, also known as the garden boa, uses its prehensile tail to cling to the branches of trees. Although not venomous, it can inflict a painful bite.

RUBBER ROBBER

The North American rubber boa lives in woodlands and meadows, where it hunts among fallen logs, in crevices, or down burrows. It also climbs trees to steal young birds from their nests. This snake looks and feels rubbery, hence its name.

RUBBER BOA

More constrictors

Pythons, from Australasia, Africa, and Asia, and anacondas, from South America, are some of the biggest snakes in the world. But despite tales of man-eating serpents, they are not large enough to devour people or any other large mammal. If a snake did eat such a meal, it would be defenseless for at least a week digesting it.

Tail acts as anchor

D'ALBERT'S WATER PYTHON

WATER PYTHON
D'Albert's water python lives in rain forests and swamps in southern New Guinea and on neighboring islands. Its dark body has no markings, except for some pale areas around the mouth. It eats mammals and birds.

LARGEST PYTHON
The reticulated python of Southeast Asia is well camouflaged for life on the forest floor. It may grow to 33 ft (10 m) in length, making it the longest snake in the world. It feeds on mammals, lizards and the occasional snake.

RETICULATED PYTHON

BLOOD PYTHON

SHORT AND BLOODY
The blood python gets its name from its colorful camouflage markings. It is also known as the short python because its tail is much shorter than those of other species. It comes from wet places in the central and southern Malay peninsula and on neighboring islands.

HUNTED FOR ITS SKIN
The Indian python lives in
a wide range of habitats,
feeding on mammals, birds,
and reptiles. It is now an
endangered species because
people have slaughtered it for
its skin and destroyed much of its
natural habitat.

*Skin is used to
make belts
and shoes*

INDIAN PYTHON

ANACONDAS

YELLOW ANACONDA

SWAMP SNAKE
The yellow anaconda lives
in swamps and marshes and
on the banks of rivers and
streams in Brazil, Bolivia,
Paraguay, and Argentina.
At 11½ ft (3.5 m) in length,
it is about half the size of
the common anaconda.

RECORD HOLDER
The common anaconda is
probably the world's largest
snake, being heavier than its rival
for the title, the reticulated python.
The average adult length is about
20 ft (6 m), although individuals of
over 26 ft (8 m) have been seen. It
is found in Trinidad and many parts
of tropical South America.

COMMON
ANACONDA

COLUBRID SNAKES

ABOUT THREE-QUARTERS of the world's snakes – over 2,000 species – belong to the colubrid family. Some are venomous, but a large number are completely harmless. Among the harmless ones are kingsnakes, water snakes, ratsnakes, the egg-eating snake, and the grass snake.

CALIFORNIA KINGSNAKE

VARIABLE PATTERNS
The colors and patterns of California kingsnakes vary greatly – individuals may be cross-banded or have stripes running down the body. Kingsnakes eat a wide range of small animals, including venomous snakes.

Markings look similar to a coral snake's

CALIFORNIA MOUNTAIN KINGSNAKE

COLUBRID FACTS
• A Japanese albino form of the yellow ratsnake is considered to be an earthly form of a fertility goddess called Benzai-ten.

• Scientists call colubrids "typical" snakes.

MOUNTAIN KINGS
California mountain kingsnakes prey on small animals, including rodents, lizards, and nestling birds. When not hunting, they often hide under stones, logs, or piles of leaves. They come from the west coast of the US.

MILK DRINKER?
The milk snake is a
species of kingsnake;
there are over 17
subspecies. The name comes
from the popular but totally
incorrect belief that they
take milk from cows. This
subspecies occurs in
Mexico, where it preys
mostly on rodents,
killing them by
constriction.

SINOLOAN MILK SNAKE

*Colored bands
mimic those of a
poisonous coral snake*

*Markings resemble
the patterns on an
ear of corn*

*Iridescent colors
give the sunbeam
snake its name*

SUNBEAM SNAKE

CORN SNAKE

NIGHT HUNTER
Like boas and
pythons, the Asian
sunbeam snake still
has the remnants of
hind limbs. It lives
in burrows in areas
where the soil is damp
and emerges at night to prey on
frogs, small mammals, and other snakes.

URBAN MYTH?
The corn snake, also called the red
ratsnake, is said to be common in the
sewers of cities in the southeastern US.

Its natural surroundings
are, in fact, woodlands,
where it preys on rodents,
bats, birds, and lizards. A
shy snake, it uses logs and
tree stumps for cover.

More colubrid snakes

Nonvenomous colubrid snakes kill either by constricting or by overpowering and swallowing the victim. For defense, they usually rely on camouflage and the ability to escape quickly. Ratsnakes, however, defend themselves by throwing the front end of their bodies into an S-shape and vibrating their tails, while bullsnakes puff themselves up to appear more formidable.

EUROPEAN WATER SNAKE

Markings look like an adder's

HARMLESS VIPER
The European water snake, also called the viperine grass snake, has warning markings that resemble those of a venomous adder. It is actually completely harmless, like all other water snakes. A good swimmer, it feeds on fish and frogs.

MOELLENDORFF'S RATSNAKE

Flowerlike patterns give this snake its Chinese name

HUNDRED FLOWERS
Moellendorff's ratsnake, known poetically as the "hundred flower snake" in Chinese, comes from southeastern China, where it feeds on rodents and birds.

COLUBRID FACTS
• Ratsnakes vibrate their tails when threatened and are often mistaken for rattlesnakes.

• In the US, farmers sometimes use bullsnakes to catch rats and mice in barns.

BAT CATCHER

The mangrove ratsnake lives in the forests of Southeast Asia. It preys on birds and small mammals, including bats, which it catches as they fly out to feed. If threatened, it inflates its body to look larger than normal.

Tail wrapped around a rock gives good anchorage

MANGROVE RATSNAKE

SPECIAL SPIKES

The egg-eating snake's backbone has about 30 ventral spikes, which are used for breaking up eggs inside the snake's body.

EGG-EATER'S SPINE   *Ventral spikes*

EGG-EATER

Egg-eating snakes are virtually toothless and have unusually elastic skins. This enables them to swallow a whole egg, which is crushed inside the body. About 15 minutes later, the snake ejects the shell remains from its mouth.

Egg may be up to three times the size of the snake's mouth

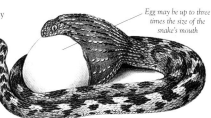

AFRICAN EGG-EATING SNAKE

VENOMOUS SNAKES

VENOM – a poisonous fluid produced by an animal – is widely used for killing or incapacitating prey. Snake venom, which is a very complex substance, serves two main purposes. First, the poison quickly subdues a prey animal, thus reducing the risk to the snake of injury from retaliation. At the same time, chemicals within the venom start to break down the prey's tissues, making digestion easier.

KING COBRA

FIXED FANGS
Cobras have fixed fangs at the front of the mouth, as do kraits, sea snakes, coral snakes, the taipan, and the tiger snake.

WARNING RATTLE
A rattlesnake is a typical front-fanged snake. As it opens its mouth, the snake rotates its fangs forward, ready to inject venom. This species is the most venomous snake in North America and feeds mainly on rats and rabbits.

Fangs are in forward position, ready to strike

Fangs normally lie flat inside the mouth

Rattle warns off predators

EASTERN DIAMONDBACK RATTLESNAKE

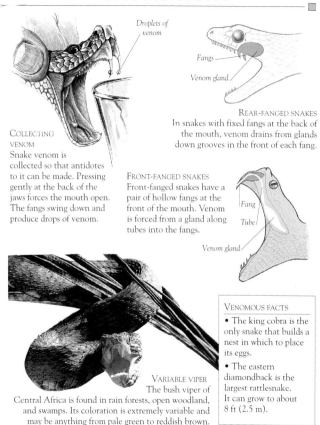

Droplets of
venom

Fangs

Venom gland

REAR-FANGED SNAKES
In snakes with fixed fangs at the back of
the mouth, venom drains from glands
down grooves in the front of each fang.

COLLECTING
VENOM
Snake venom is
collected so that antidotes
to it can be made. Pressing
gently at the back of the
jaws forces the mouth open.
The fangs swing down and
produce drops of venom.

FRONT-FANGED SNAKES
Front-fanged snakes have a
pair of hollow fangs at the
front of the mouth. Venom
is forced from a gland along
tubes into the fangs.

Fang

Tube

Venom gland

VENOMOUS FACTS
• The king cobra is the
only snake that builds a
nest in which to place
its eggs.
• The eastern
diamondback is the
largest rattlesnake.
It can grow to about
8 ft (2.5 m).

VARIABLE VIPER
The bush viper of
Central Africa is found in rain forests, open woodland,
and swamps. Its coloration is extremely variable and
may be anything from pale green to reddish brown.

REAR-FANGED SNAKES

SNAKES WITH FANGS in the back of their mouth are
found in both the Old and New Worlds, and, as with
other groups of snakes, they vary greatly in color,
size, and habitat. They are not as efficient as front-
fanged snakes at injecting venom,
and so most species are harmless to
humans. Large rear-fanged snakes,
however, can be dangerous.

CORAL MIMIC
The false coral snake
preys on lizards, small
mammals, and
other small
snakes. It is found
in the forests of
Central America, from
Venezuela to Costa Rica.

FALSE CORAL SNAKE

*Colors
resemble those of a
more dangerous snake*

MANGROVE SNAKE
In the mangrove swamps of the Malay
Peninsula this large snake – adults grow
to over 6½ ft (2 m) – preys on a wide
variety of small animals. The seven
subspecies of mangrove snake have
different numbers of yellow bands.

LIZARD HUNTER
The blunt-headed tree snake is found in trees and shrubs from southern Mexico to Bolivia and Paraguay. It is active by night and feeds mostly on lizards such as anoles and geckos.

BLUNT-HEADED TREE SNAKE

PARROT SNAKE

Gaping mouth is a warning to enemies

IDLE THREAT
When threatened, a parrot snake raises its head and opens its mouth, but rarely strikes. Slender and well camouflaged, it hunts lizards and amphibians in the dense foliage of the rain forests of Central and South America.

This snake often feeds on eggs laid on leaves by frogs

CAT EYES
The green cat-eyed snake lives in the forests of northeastern India, where it hunts at night for frogs, lizards, and small birds.

Camouflaged for life in the treetops

GREEN CAT-EYED SNAKE

More rear-fanged snakes

The venom produced by rear-fanged snakes is just as lethal as that of front-fanged snakes, and in some cases is specific to a particular prey. For example, the venom of a snake that usually eats frogs may be more toxic to frogs than to other animals, such as mice. The venom of both the boomslang and the twigsnake has occasionally killed people.

HOG-NOSED BURROWER
The Madagascan giant hognose snake eats birds and small mammals. It shelters in rock crevices, beneath debris, or in burrows that it digs. It lives in grassland and grows to about 5 ft (1.5 m) in length.

When threatened, this snake flattens its neck like a cobra and hisses loudly

MADAGASCAN GIANT HOGNOSE SNAKE

SONORAN LYRE SNAKE

REAR-FANGED FACTS
• The mussurana first constricts its prey, and then injects venom into it.
• The Australasian brown tree snake, introduced into Guam, has caused the decline of many native birds.

LYRE HEAD
Lyre snakes get their name from the lyre-shaped marking on the head. They live in rocky places in California, Arizona, and Mexico, feeding on lizards, small birds, and mammals. They are nocturnal.

FROG-EATER

The night snake, also known locally as the cat-eyed snake, is found in Mexico and Central America. It spends much of its time in trees and hunts at night for frogs and lizards.

NIGHT SNAKE
EATING FROGS' EGGS

Vine snake hangs from a branch, waiting for prey

VINE CREEPER

The vine snake's camouflage allows it to creep unseen among bushes and vines. Native to brush-covered hillsides in Mexico and Arizona, it preys mainly on lizards, and occasionally on small birds and nestlings.

MEXICAN
VINE SNAKE

BOOMSLANG

The African boomslang moves with speed and grace through woodland, scrub, savannah, and swamp. It eats birds' eggs and also uses its quick-acting venom to kill small mammals, frogs, and birds. Its name is Afrikaans for "tree snake."

FRONT FANGS

FRONT-FANGED SNAKES, such as cobras, can inject venom into almost any animal, making them among the most dangerous of all reptiles. As with all venomous snakes, their venom is normally used for killing or disabling prey, but it is equally effective as a defense. However, most snakes usually prefer to escape rather than attack a predator.

HORUS
The Egyptian sky god, Horus, demonstrates his dominion over reptiles by grasping snakes and standing on a crocodile.

COBRA FACTS
• Every year, thousands of Asian cobras are killed for their skins.
• The king cobra is the world's largest venomous snake – individuals exceeding 16 ft (5 m) in length have been recorded.

Cobra rears up before spitting

RED SPITTING COBRA

VENOM SPITTER
A spitting cobra has a very effective method of defense. When threatened, and with no means of escape, it rears up and squirts a jet of poison into the attacker's eyes, causing severe pain and even permanent blindness.

MARK OF BUDDHA

The Asian cobra has a characteristic "eye" or "monocle" on its hood. This is said to be the fingerprint of Buddha, who blessed this snake after it had shaded him as he slept in the desert.

MONOCLED COBRA

"Eye" is meant to frighten aggressors

Cobras are active at dawn and dusk

Some snake charmers remove the cobra's fangs

Cobras follow the instrument's movements

SNAKE CHARMER AND COBRAS

HOODED MENACE

Most cobras have a hood, created by spreading the neck ribs as the front of the body is raised off the ground. This characteristic is particularly well developed in Asian species, such as the Ceylonese cobra.

A cobra can move forward while keeping its front raised

CHARMED SNAKES

Snake charmers in Asia and North Africa have long induced cobras to "dance" to their tunes. The snakes, however, are deaf and are probably reacting to the swaying movements of the instrument, not to the music.

The hood is spread as the body is raised

CEYLONESE COBRA

Vipers

With their long, hollow fangs, vipers and their close relatives, the pit vipers and rattlesnakes, are among the most dangerous snakes in the world. When one of these snakes opens its mouth to bite, it swings its fangs downward and forward, ready to stab the victim. The snake has absolute control over the movement of its fangs – it can even choose to erect them one at a time.

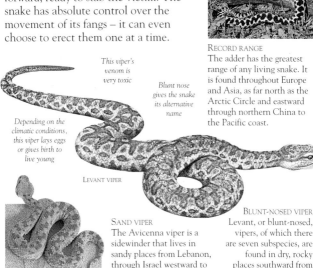

RECORD RANGE
The adder has the greatest range of any living snake. It is found throughout Europe and Asia, as far north as the Arctic Circle and eastward through northern China to the Pacific coast.

This viper's venom is very toxic

Blunt nose gives the snake its alternative name

Depending on the climatic conditions, this viper lays eggs or gives birth to live young

LEVANT VIPER

AVICENNA VIPER

SAND VIPER
The Avicenna viper is a sidewinder that lives in sandy places from Lebanon, through Israel westward to the northwestern coast of Africa. It is closely related to the horned viper.

BLUNT-NOSED VIPER
Levant, or blunt-nosed, vipers, of which there are seven subspecies, are found in dry, rocky places southward from Georgia to northern Israel, Iraq, Iran, and a few of the Greek islands.

YELLOW PERIL
The eyelash viper has spiny scales above its eyes that resemble eyelashes. This tree-dwelling pit viper is found in rain forests from southern Mexico southward to Ecuador and western Venezuela. It varies in color from brown or green to lemon yellow.

EYELASH VIPER

LOOKS LIKE A VIPER . . .
The death, or deaf, adder looks and behaves like a viper, but is related to the cobras, coral snakes, and kraits. It lives in dry, sandy places in Australia, New Guinea, and nearby islands.

DEATH ADDER

ALL PUFFED UP
A good climber and swimmer, the puff adder is found in all habitats except deserts in Africa south of the Sahara. It preys on a wide variety of animals and, like all vipers, prefers to lie in wait for its victims. The puff adder's venom is highly toxic.

Grey and brown coloring for camouflage in dry grass

PUFF ADDER

Rattlesnakes

The distinctive feature of these well-known, front-fanged snakes is the rattle at the end of the tail, which is made of a series of special, ringlike scales. Rattlesnakes, all of which are found in the southern half of North America, are under threat, mainly from excessive slaughter by hunters, together with the continued spread of agriculture and urban development. All rattlesnakes give birth to live young.

SOUTHERN PACIFIC
RATTLESNAKE

ADAPTABLE
The southern Pacific rattlesnake is found in rocky and sandy environments. An adaptable species, it can also survive in urban and agricultural areas. It preys mainly on rodents.

EASTERN
DIAMONDBACK
RATTLESNAKE

RATTLESNAKE FACTS
• Organized hunts called "rattlesnake roundups" in the US have wiped out many local populations.

• Western diamondbacks always return to the same den to hibernate.

LARGE – BUT SECRETIVE
The eastern diamondback is a secretive reptile found in pine and oak woods and abandoned agricultural areas. It is a large, heavy-bodied snake that preys on small mammals, particularly rabbits and rats.

VARIED HABITATS
Black-tailed rattlesnakes are found in Mexico, Arizona, and Texas, usually in rocky places and sometimes in woodland and open grassland. They may be active at any time of the day, and they prey on small rodents.

Diamond-shaped, pale-bordered blotches

WESTERN
DIAMONDBACK
RATTLESNAKE

LARGE GATHERINGS
Western diamondbacks can be found in a variety of dry habitats in Mexico and the southern US. They hibernate in the autumn, gathering in large numbers in suitable den sites. They feed on small mammals and birds.

A diamondback will defend itself vigorously if cornered

DUSKY PGYMY RATTLESNAKE

PYGMY RATTLER
The dusky pygmy rattlesnake lives in dry, sandy places near water. It is active at any time of the day or night, and it preys on small animals, including small snakes and large insects. It grows to only about 20 in (50 cm) in length.

Other front-fanged snakes

Front-fanged snakes that have fixed fangs include the tiger snake, the taipan, kraits, and sea snakes. Unlike true vipers and rattlesnakes, these snakes cannot stab their prey with their fangs and must actually bite. The cottonmouth and its close relatives, the moccasin and the copperhead, are pit vipers and are thus members of the Crotalinae, the viper subfamily that includes the rattlesnakes.

BANDED SEA SNAKE

TIGER SNAKE

SEA SERPENT
Sea snakes include the world's most venomous snakes. Luckily, the banded sea snakes, of which five species live in coastal waters around New Guinea and Pacific islands, seldom bite in defense.

TOXIC TIGER
The venom of southern Australia's tiger snake is highly toxic – just 3 mg is enough to kill a human. It feeds mainly on frogs, but also kills small mammals and lizards. The tiger snake is quick to attack if disturbed.

NEVER FATAL
The American copperhead is found in open woodland, where it feeds on mice, birds, frogs, and insects. Contrary to popular belief, its bite is never fatal, although this has not stopped the widespread killing of these snakes.

Copperheads hibernate in communal dens

COPPERHEAD

TURTLE EATER

The cottonmouth, also called the water moccasin, is an impressive-looking, heavy-bodied snake that lives in swamps and marshes in Alabama, Georgia, and Virginia. Its prey includes small turtles and young alligators.

COTTONMOUTH

Taipans shelter in mammal burrows and rock crevices, or under piles of forest litter

TAIPAN

DO NOT DISTURB

The taipan is a large, slender snake found in northern Australia. When not hunting, it seeks shelter and, whenever possible, will retreat when disturbed. If cornered, however, it becomes fearsomely aggressive.

Prey consists of small mammals

Taipan is one of Australia's most dangerous snakes

COMMON KRAIT

The common, or blue, krait is a highly venomous snake found in the dry woodland plains and meadows of Bangladesh, India, and Sri Lanka. It hides during the day and at night hunts rodents, lizards, and other snakes.

FRONT-FANGED FACTS

• A cottonmouth uses its bright yellow tail as a lure to attract prey.

• A bite from a krait is fatal in over 75 percent of cases.

• Some species of sea snake are considered to be a delicacy in the Far East.

REFERENCE SECTION

REPTILE CLASSIFICATION

REPTILES ARE DIVIDED into six subclasses, but only three of them contain living species. The tuatara, lizards, and snakes make up the largest living group. Groups marked with an asterisk (*) are extinct.

CLASS: REPTILIA

SUBCLASS: ANAPSIDA

ORDER: COTYLOSAURIA (Stem reptiles)*

ORDER: MESOSAURIA (Mesosaurus)*

ORDER: CHELONIA

Suborder: Cryptodira

Family: Carettochelyidae (New Guinea plateless turtle)
Family: Cheloniidae (Sea turtles)
Family: Dermochelyidae (Leatherback turtle)
Family: Chelydridae (Snapping turtles)
Family: Dermatemydidae (Central American river turtle)
Family: Emydidae (Map turtles, box turtles, sliders, roofed turtles, wood turtles, pond turtles, painted turtle, chicken turtle, snake-eating turtle, Indian black turtle, bog turtle, and others)
Family: Kinosternidae (Mud turtles, musk turtles)
Family: Platysternidae (Big-headed turtle)
Family: Testudinae (Tortoises)
Family: Trionychidae (Soft-shelled turtles)

STARRED TORTOISE
Like all land tortoises, the starred tortoise belongs to the family Testudinae. It and its relatives are classified with the most primitive reptiles.

Suborder: Pleurodira

Family: Chelidae (Snake-necked turtles, matamata)
Family: Pelomedusidae (Afro-American sidenecks)

SUBCLASS: SYNAPTOSAURIA

ORDER: PROTEROSAURIA (Tanystropheus and others)*

ORDER: SAUROPTERYGIA (Pliosaurs, plesiosaurs)*

ORDER: PLACODONTIA (Placodonts)*

SUBCLASS: ICHTHYOPTERYGIA

ORDER: ICHTHYOSAURIDAE (Ichythyosaurs)*

SUBCLASS: ARCHOSAURIA

ORDER: THECODONTIA (Thecodonts)*

ORDER: SAURISCHIA (Theropods and sauropods)*

ORDER: ORNITHISCHIA (Ornithopods, stegosaurs, ankylosaurs, ceratopsians)*

ORDER: PTEROSAURIA (Pterosaurs)*

ORDER: CROCODILIA

Family: Crocodylidae (Crocodiles)
Family: Alligatoridae (Alligators and caimans)
Family: Gavialidae (Gharial)

NILE CROCODILE
Crocodilians are the only living members of the Archosauria, the "ruling reptiles."

SUBCLASS: SYNAPSIDA (Mammal-like reptiles)*

SUBCLASS: LEPIDOSAURIA

ORDER: EOSUCHIA (Early lizards)*

ORDER: RHYNCHOCEPHALIA
(Early rhyncocephalians*, tuatara)

TUATARA
The tuatara's unusual
skull shows that it is
the last surviving
rhynchocephalian.

ORDER: SQUAMATA

Suborder: Lacertilia

Family: Gekkonidae (Geckos)
Family: Pygopodidae (Snake lizards)
Family: Iguanidae (Iguanas, anoles, basilisks, spiny lizards, horned lizards)
Family: Agamidae (Agamas, flying lizards, garden lizards, bearded dragons,
    frilled lizard, moloch, spring-tailed lizards, water dragons)
Family: Chamaeleonidae (Chameleons)
Family: Lacertidae (Wall lizards, common lizard, eyed lizard, sand lizard,
    oriental long-tailed lizard, and many others)
Family: Teiidae (Whiptails, tegus, caiman lizards, and others)
Family: Xantusiidae (Night lizards)
Family: Scincidae (Skinks, sandfish)
Family: Cordylidae (Girdle-tailed lizards, plated lizards, crag lizards,
    flat lizards, armadillo lizard)
Family: Dibamidae (Blind lizards)
Family: Anguidae (Slow worm, glass lizards, alligator lizards,
    and others)
Family: Anniellidae (Legless lizards)
Family: Xenosauridae (Xenosaurs, Chinese crocodile lizard)
Family: Varanidae (Monitors)
Family: Helodermatidae (Beaded lizard, Gila monster)
Family: Lanthonotidae (Bornean earless monitor)

GECKO
Geckos make up one of the
largest lizard families –
there are about 830 species.

Suborder: Amphisbaena (Worm lizards)

Family: Amphisbaenidae (120 legless species)
Family: Trogonophidae (six legless species)
Family: Rhineuridae (one legless species)
Family: Bipedidae (Ajolote and two other species
    with front limbs)

Suborder: Ophidia

Family: Uropeltidae (Shield-tailed snakes)
Family: Xenopeltidae (Sunbeam snakes)
Family: Leptotyphlopidae (Thread snakes)
Family: Typhlopidae (Blind snakes)
Family: Boidae (Boas, pythons, anaconda)
Family: Achrochordidae (Wart snakes)
Family: Colubridae (Ratsnakes, corn snake, parrot snake, whipsnakes, racers,
    bullsnakes, kingsnakes, milk snakes, water snakes, grass snake, egg-eating
    snakes, smooth snake, hognose snakes, Mexican long-nosed snake, mangrove
    snake, mussurana, boomslang, false coral snake, parrot snake, Mexican vine
    snake, lyre snake, cat-eyed snakes, night snake, blunt-headed tree snake,
    brown tree snake, twig snake, and others)
Family: Elapidae (Cobras, black mamba, kraits, coral
    snakes, death adder, tiger snake, taipan, sea snakes)
Family: Viperidae
  Subfamily: Azemiopinae (one rare species)
  Subfamily: Viperinae (True vipers, adders,
    asp)
  Subfamily: Crotalinae (Pit vipers,
    moccasins, copperheads, amur viper,
    cottonmouths, sharp-nosed viper,
    Indian tree viper, palm vipers,
    fer-de-lance, bushmaster, western
    hog-nosed viper, rattlesnakes,
    sidewinders)

WORM LIZARD
There are some 130 species
of amphisbaenians, or worm
lizards. They are wormlike,
burrowing animals.

RATSNAKE
Ratsnakes are among
the many nonvenomous
species that belong to
the family Colubridae.

REPTILES AS PETS

REPTILES ARE WILD ANIMALS, so keeping them is not as simple as looking after a dog. Learn as much as you can before buying: find out the reptile's adult size, its temperament, its living conditions. And always bear in mind that *all* reptiles should be handled with care, not just the poisonous species.

CLEANING AND HANDLING REPTILES

CLEANING A TERRAPIN
Algae can build up on a terrapin's shell. To remove it, hold the animal gently and scrub the shell lightly with a toothbrush. Wash your hands afterward, as all reptiles can carry diseases.

Gently brush off the algae

PICKING UP A SNAKE
Most snakes, even non-poisonous ones, may bite if handled carelessly. If you are unsure of the snake, pin the head gently but firmly to the ground and grasp it just behind the head.

HANDLING A SNAKE
When handling a snake, it is important to support the whole body. A venomous snake should be held firmly behind the head; non-venomous species can be allowed to glide around your arms, hands, and body.

Frequent handling helps a snake become less afraid

HOW TO HOUSE REPTILES

SELECTING THE RIGHT CAGE

For small snakes and lizards, a simple glass-fronted box or cage is usually adequate. It should provide warmth and a good circulation of air, be easy to see into, and free from rough surfaces, such as wire mesh.

A TERRAPIN TANK

Terrapins can be kept successfully in a plain glass aquarium tank. Arrange rocks and other materials, such as small flowerpots, to make it possible for the animals to get out of the water and onto "dry land." Remember to change the water regularly and to remove any excess food scraps.

LANDSCAPING THE CAGE

Line the cage with a suitable material, such as newspaper, earth, or sand, and add a tree branch for climbing species.

KEEPING REPTILES WELL FED

It is vital to know a reptile's correct feeding requirements. Snakes normally eat live food, but in a small cage a live animal may be regarded by the snake as a threat, triggering a defense response rather than a feeding one. Feeding with freshly killed animals is an alternative that many snakes will accept. Herbivores, such as tortoises, need a supply of fresh plant material.

Vitamins and minerals are an essential part of any animal's diet – red-eared terrapins, for example, often fail to reach maturity if their food lacks them – and supplements may be needed.

All tortoises are plant-eaters

REPTILE RECORDS

FROM THE WORLD'S LONGEST-LIVED ANIMAL to the largest creature that ever existed, reptiles are natural record breakers. The following is a selection of amazing reptile records.

LARGEST REPTILE
The largest reptile, the estuarine crocodile, may grow to over 23 ft (7 m) in length.

ESTUARINE CROCODILE

OLDEST REPTILE
A Madagascan radiated tortoise is known to have lived for over 188 years.

SHORTEST SNAKE
The rare thread snake, which lives only on the islands of Martinique, St. Lucia, and Barbados, seems to have a maximum length of just over 4½ in (11.5 cm).

OLDEST LIZARD
A slow worm in the Zoological Museum in Copenhagen lived for over 54 years. It died in 1946.

RAREST REPTILE
The rarest reptile is the short-necked swamp tortoise of western Australia, which has an estimated wild population of 20 to 25.

FASTEST REPTILE
The highest speed recorded for a land reptile is 21.7 mph (34.9 km/h), achieved by a spiny-tailed iguana in a series of experiments carried out by a scientist in Costa Rica.

OLDEST SNAKE
A male common boa constrictor called Popeye died in 1977 aged 40 years, 3 months, and 14 days at the Philadelphia Zoo.

FASTEST IN WATER
It is said that a frightened leatherback turtle achieved a speed of 22 mph (35 km/h), the highest speed claimed for any reptile in water.

LARGEST LIZARD
The Komodo dragon is the largest lizard. One measured 10 ft, 2 in (3.1 m) from head to tail.

KOMODO DRAGON

LARGEST CHELONIANS

The largest chelonian is the leatherback turtle. One specimen was 9 ft, 5½ in (2.9 m) in length and weighed 2,120 lb (961 kg). The largest known Galápagos giant tortoise lives at the Life Fellowship Bird sanctuary in Florida. It weighs 849 lb (385 kg).

LEATHERBACK
TURTLE

FASTEST SNAKE

The black mamba of Africa is reputed to be the fastest-moving land snake. It can probably reach 10–12 mph (14–19 km/h) in short bursts.

MOST VENOMOUS SNAKES

The venom of the sea snake *Hydrophis belcheri* is estimated to be a hundred times as toxic as that of a taipan. The most venomous land snake is the small-scaled, or fierce, snake of Australia.

LARGEST DINOSAUR

The largest land animals were sauropod dinosaurs. One of the largest, *Brachiosaurus*, was 70 ft (22 m) long and 39 ft (12 m) high, and weighed about 77 tons (70 tonnes).

OLDEST CROCODILIAN

A female American alligator at Adelaide Zoo, Australia, died in 1978 at the age of 66 years.

LARGEST SNAKES

The longest snake recorded was a 32 ft, 10 in (10 m) long reticulated python killed in 1912 on the island of Celebes. The heaviest snake is the anaconda of South America and Trinidad. The longest recorded one measured 27 ft, 9 in (8.5 m) and is estimated to have weighed about 500 lb (227 kg). The longest venomous snake is the

RETICULATED
PYTHON

king cobra of Southeast Asia. In the 1930s, one specimen grew to 18 ft, 9 in (5.7 m) at the London Zoo.

SMALLEST REPTILE

The smallest reptile is the British Virgin Islands gecko, shown below on the hand of a ten-year-old child. It grows to a maximum length of just ⁷⁄₁₀ in (18 mm).

BRITISH
VIRGIN
ISLANDS
GECKO

Glossary

AMPHIBIAN
An egg-laying vertebrate animal that either lives in water or must return to water to breed.

ARBOREAL
Lives in trees.

BLUFF
A form of defense that creates the impression that an animal is more dangerous than it really is.

BRILLE
See Spectacle.

CAMOUFLAGE
A combination of coloring and pattern that allows an animal to blend in with its surroundings.

CARAPACE
The upper part of the shell of a turtle or tortoise.

CARTILAGINOUS
Made of cartilage, a tough tissue that protects the bones of most vertebrates.

CENOZOIC ERA
The period of time on the geological time scale that covers from 65 million years ago to the present day.

COLD-BLOODED
Having a body temperature that is dependent on the outside temperature.

CONSTRICTION
Killing prey by coiling round it and squeezing it until it suffocates.

ECTOTHERMS
Cold-blooded animals; see Poikilotherms.

EGG
Structure produced by insects, reptiles, and birds that enables an embryo to develop on land without the need for water as a growth medium.

EMBRYO
The stage of development from the time a fertilized egg cell (ovum) starts to divide to the point of hatching.

ENDANGERED
A species in danger of becoming extinct due to human activity.

EXTINCT
A species that no longer exists, due to either natural causes or the activities of humans.

HABITAT
The local part of the environment preferred as a living area by one or more species.

HERBIVOROUS
An animal that lives exclusively on plant material.

INCUBATE
Maintain at a suitable temperature for the time needed for an embryo to develop into a hatchling.

IRIDESCENCE
Rainbowlike colors produced by the diffraction of light from a surface rather than pigments within the material.

JURASSIC PERIOD
The period of time on the geological time scale that lasted from 190 to 135 million years ago.

MIMICRY
The adoption of colors that resemble those of another dangerous or unpalatable species.

OSSIFIED
Partly or completely converted into bone material.

PELVIC GIRDLE
The hip girdle. The arrangement of bones in the hip region that connects the leg bones to the vertebral column.

PINEAL BODY
Light-sensitive outgrowth of the front part of the brain. Present in fishes and amphibians; also in reptiles, in which the front part forms an eye-like structure. Thought to be involved in reproduction and the control of an animal's daily internal rhythms.

PLASTRON
The lower part of the shell of a turtle or tortoise.

POIKILOTHERMS
A "cold-blooded" animal whose body temperature follows that of the surrounding environment.

PREDATOR
An animal that preys on other animals.

PREHENSILE TAIL
A tail that can grasp; usually used for holding on to branches.

PREY
An animal that is killed and eaten by a predator.

REPTILE
An egg-laying land vertebrate with a tough or scaly skin. Living forms include the chelonians, crocodilians, lizards, snakes, and tuatara.

SCUTE
A horny shield on the shells of turtles and tortoises.

SPECIES
A group of animals that can normally interbreed only with each other.

SPECTACLE
Transparent membrane on the front of a snake's eye. Also known as the brille in lizards.

THECODONTS
A group of Triassic lizardlike reptiles that gave rise to the dinosaurs, crocodilians, pterosaurs, and birds.

TRIASSIC PERIOD
The period of time on the geological time scale that lasted from 230 to 190 million years ago.

VENOM
Fluid containing a poisonous substance that rapidly incapacitates or kills.

VENOMOUS
An animal that incapacitates or kills its prey by the use of venom.

VENTRAL
Relating to the front part of an animal. Conventionally the side that normally faces downward; the opposite side to dorsal, the side that normally faces upward.

WARNING COLORS
Colors that warn predators of an animal's unpalatability or ability to defend itself with poison.

YOLK SAC
The saclike structure in an egg that contains the food store, or yolk.

Resources

Reading about reptiles will definitely increase your knowledge of them, but nothing beats seeing reptiles in the flesh. Listed below are zoos with very good reptile collections.

UNITED STATES
Arizona–Sonora Desert Museum
2021 North Kinney Road
Tucson, Arizona 85743
(602) 883-1380

Audubon Park and Zoological Garden
6500 Magazine Street
New Orleans,
Louisiana 70118
(504) 861-2537

Baltimore Zoo
Druid Hill Park
Baltimore,
Maryland 21217
(410) 396-7102

Buffalo Zoological Garden
Delaware Park
Buffalo, New York 14214
(716) 837-3900

Busch Gardens
3605 Bougainvillea Drive
Tampa, Florida 33612
(813) 987-5250

Chicago Zoological Park
3300 Golf Road
Brookfield, Illinois 60513
(708) 485-0263

Cincinnati Zoo and Botanical Garden
3400 Vine Street
Cincinnati, Ohio 45220
(513) 281-4701

Dallas Zoo
621 East Clarendon Drive
Dallas, Texas 75203
(214) 670-6825

Honolulu Zoo
151 Kapahulu Avenue
Honolulu, Hawaii 96815
(808) 971-7174

Houston Zoological Garden
1513 North MacGregor
Houston, Texas 77030
(713) 525-3300

Indianapolis Zoo
1200 West Washington Street
Indianapolis,
Indiana 46222
(317) 630-2001

Knoxville Zoological Garden
3333 Woodbine Avenue
Knoxville,
Tennessee 37914
(615) 637-5331

Lincoln Park Zoological Garden
2200 North Cannon Drive
Chicago, Illinois 60614
(312) 294-4662

Los Angeles Zoo
5333 Zoo Drive
Los Angeles,
California 90027
(213) 666-4650

Louisville Zoological Garden
1100 Trevillian Way
Louisville,
Kentucky 40213
(502) 459-2181

Lowry Park Zoological Garden
7530 North Boulevard
Tampa, Florida 33604
(813) 935-8552

Miami Metrozoo
12400 SW 152nd Street
Miami, Florida 33177
(305) 251-0401

National Zoological Park
3000 block of
Connecticut Avenue
Washington, D.C. 20009
(202) 673-4821

New York Zoological Society
185th Street and
Southern Boulevard
Bronx, New York 10460
(718) 220-5100

Oklahoma City Zoological Park
2101 NE 50th Street
Oklahoma City,
Oklahoma 73111
(405) 424-3344

Philadelphia Zoological Garden
3400 West Girard Avenue
Philadelphia,
Pennsylvania 19104
(215) 243-1100

Rio Grand Zoological Park
903 Tenth Street SW
Albuquerque,
New Mexico 87102
(505) 843-7413

St. Augustine Alligator Farm
999 Anastasia Boulevard
St. Augustine,
Florida 32085
(904) 824-3337

St. Louis Zoological Park
Forest Park
St. Louis, Missouri 63110
(314) 781-0900

San Antonio Zoological Garden
3903 North St. Mary's
Street
San Antonio,
Texas 78212
(512) 734-7184

San Diego Zoo
Zoo Place and Park
Boulevard
Balboa Park
San Diego,
California 92103
(619) 231-1515

CANADA
Jardin Zoologique de Granby
347 rue Bourget
Granby, Quebec J2G 1E8
(514) 372-9113

Metropolitan Toronto Zoo
Meadowvale Road
Toronto, Ontario
M1E 4RS
(416) 392-5901

Index

Acknowledgments

Dorling Kindersley would like to thank:
Mark Lambert for the index; Earl Neish
and Robin Hunter for design assistance;
Caroline Potts for picture library services.

Photographs by:
Jane Burton, Geoff Dann, Mike Dunning,
Frank Greenaway, Colin Keates, Dave
King, Karl Shone, Kim Taylor, and
Jerry Young.

Illustrations by:
Janet Allis, John Hutchison, Aziz Khan,
Sallie Alane Reason, John Woodcock,
and Colin Woolf.

Picture Credits
t=top, b=bottom, c=center, l=left,
r=right.
The publisher would like to thank the
following for their kind permission to
reproduce their photographs:
Ardea: M. Krishnan 109bl; Eric Lingren
90tl.
BBC Natural History Unit: Galleria
Degli Uffizi, Florence 12tl.
Bridgeman Art Library: 58tl, 85br.
Centaur Studios: 19bl.
Lester Cheeseman: 103c.
Bruce Coleman: 81bc; Erwin & Peggy
Bauer 64tl; Fred Bruemmer 49bl; John
Cancalosi 88tl; Michael Fogden 82–3;
Michael McCoy 89tl.
FLPA: L. Chance 89bl.
John Holmes: 19cl.

Natural History Museum, London: 14cl,
14bl, 14br, 15tl, 16t, 16b, 17t, 17c, 17br,
21c, 23tl, 60bl, 60cl, 63cl, 64bl, 65t, 68b,
69t, 71tl, 73cr, 73br, 74tl, 75b, 76t, 76bl,
77br, 78b, 79t, 80–1, 80cr, 80b, 81c, 81t,
85t, 89tl, 93cr, 95br, 100r, 104bl, 108b.
Natural Science Photos: C Banks 71cr,
108tr, 108cl; C. Dani & I. Jeske 55br,
71bl; G. Kinns 98cl; J. G. Lilley 50c,
50b; Chris Mattison 77t, 98br; Jim Merli
20cr, 24bc, 32cl, 37tr, 107tl, 105t, 109cr;
Pete Oxford 49tl, 51bl; PhotoSafari
(Pvt) Ltd 110–1; Queensland Museum
105c; Richard Revels 104tr; C. & T.
Stuart 101bl.
NHPA: Daniel Heuclin 97bl; Gerard
Lacz 65cr; E. Hanumantha Rao 96cl;
Martin Wendler 91c.
Oxford Scientific Films: 40cl; Mark
Deeble & Victoria Stone 61cr; John
Downer 62br; Michael Fogden 63tr,
101tr; Tui de Roy 30cr; Alastair Shay
99cr; Maurice Tibbles 33c.
Planet Earth: Brian Kenney 84t, 88bl,
90bl, 107bl.
Wild Images: Romulus Whitaker 37br;
62tr.

Every effort has been made to trace the
copyright holders and we apologize in
advance for any unintentional omissions.
We should be pleased to insert the
appropriate acknowledgment in any
subsequent edition of this publication.